American Textbook Reading

Social Studies 1

Table of Contents

Lesson Guide

Visual Summary

The visual summary uses images with key vocabulary and other related words to introduce the main concept of the lesson. The visual summary is also an aid for word association, reinforcing the meaning of the words within context.

Title

This is what the lesson is about.

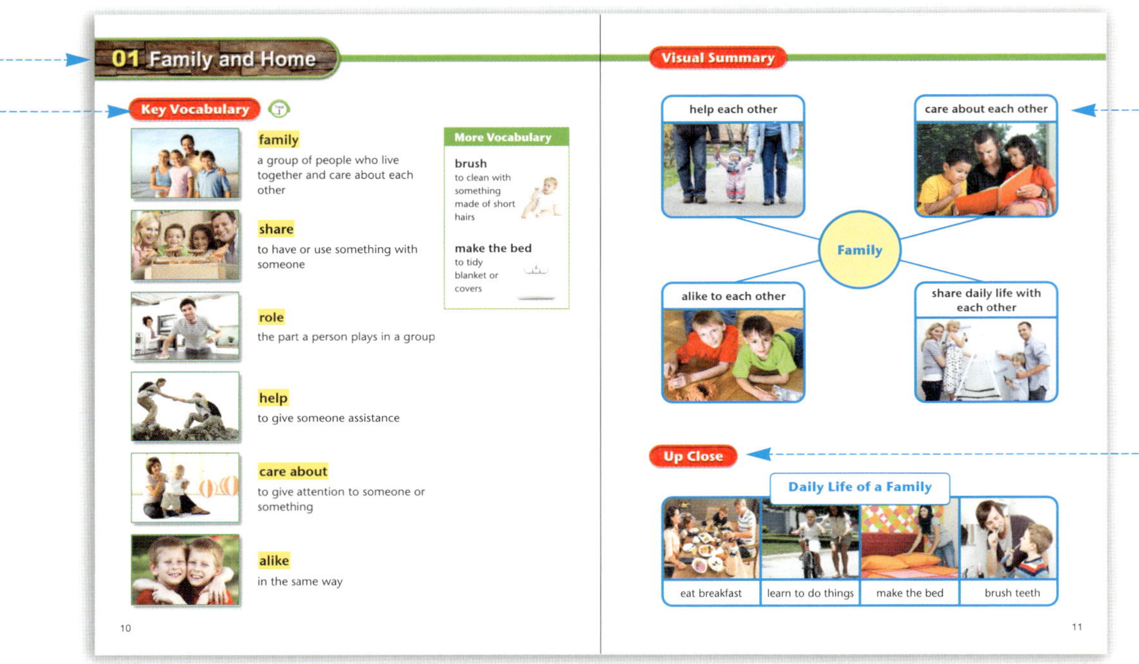

Key Vocabulary

These are new words for students to learn in the lesson.
The meaning of each word is below it.

Up Close

This expands the key vocabulary and the lesson's main idea. This gives students a greater level of understanding.

Review 1

Here there are pictures of objects or situations. Students can use a visual guide to help them remember a word.

Exercise

This exercise will test students' understanding of the written definition of the key vocabulary.

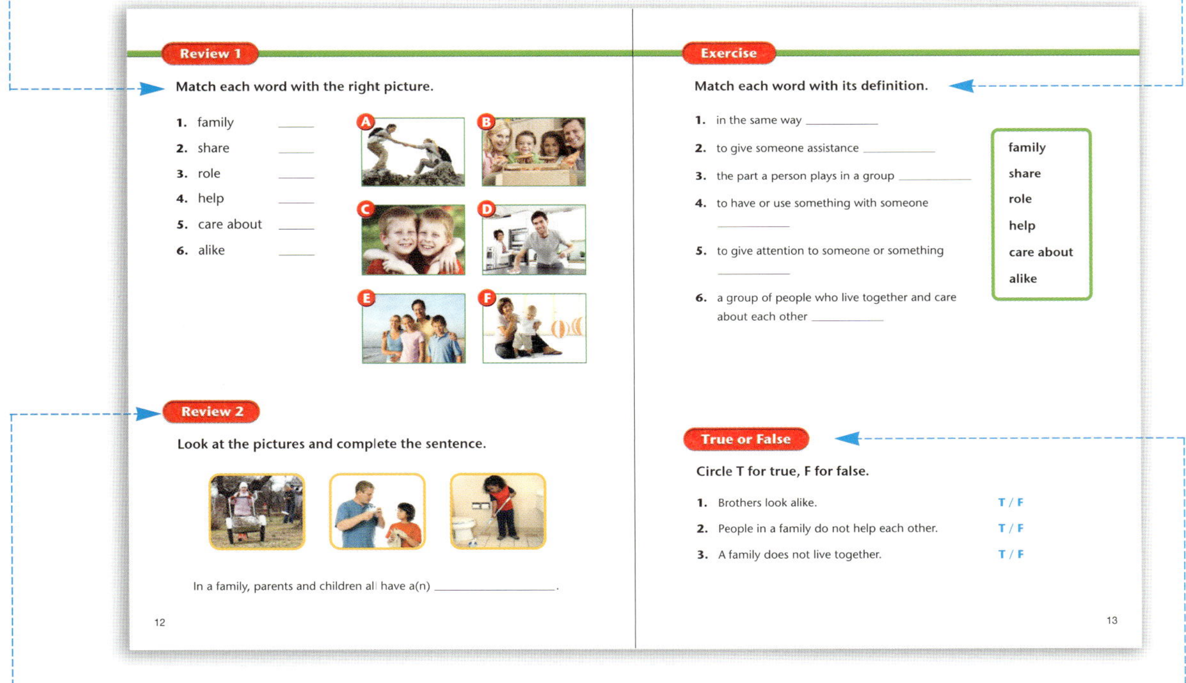

Review 2

Here there are new pictures that relate to the key vocabulary. Different pictures help students learn a new word and remember it.

True or False

This exercise make the students think carefully about a statement.

Reading

The passage is the main part of the lesson. It contains all the key vocabulary and other words students have been learning in this lesson. Students have been preparing for the passage in the previous pages. This makes it easier for students to comprehend the passage.

Comprehension

These questions test students' comprehension of the passage. They also test students' ability to remember what is written in the passage.

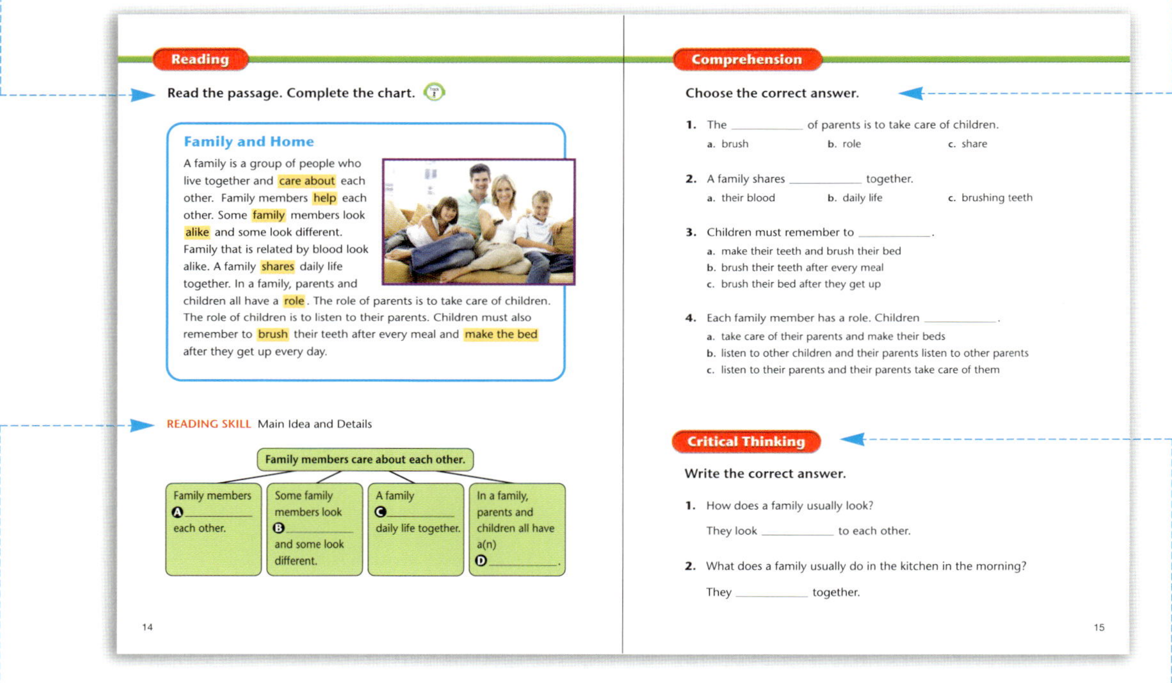

Reading Skill

Each passage follows a reading skill such as *Main Idea*, *Sequence*, *Compare* and *Contrast*, *Classify*, etc. The chart helps students identify and understand the key concepts or key parts of the passage. This aids comprehension.

Critical Thinking

These questions make students use critical thinking, which is an important part of the learning process. This section will help students develop their reading skills.

Vocabulary 1

These exercises test students' ability to remember the meaning of a word using a picture as a guide.

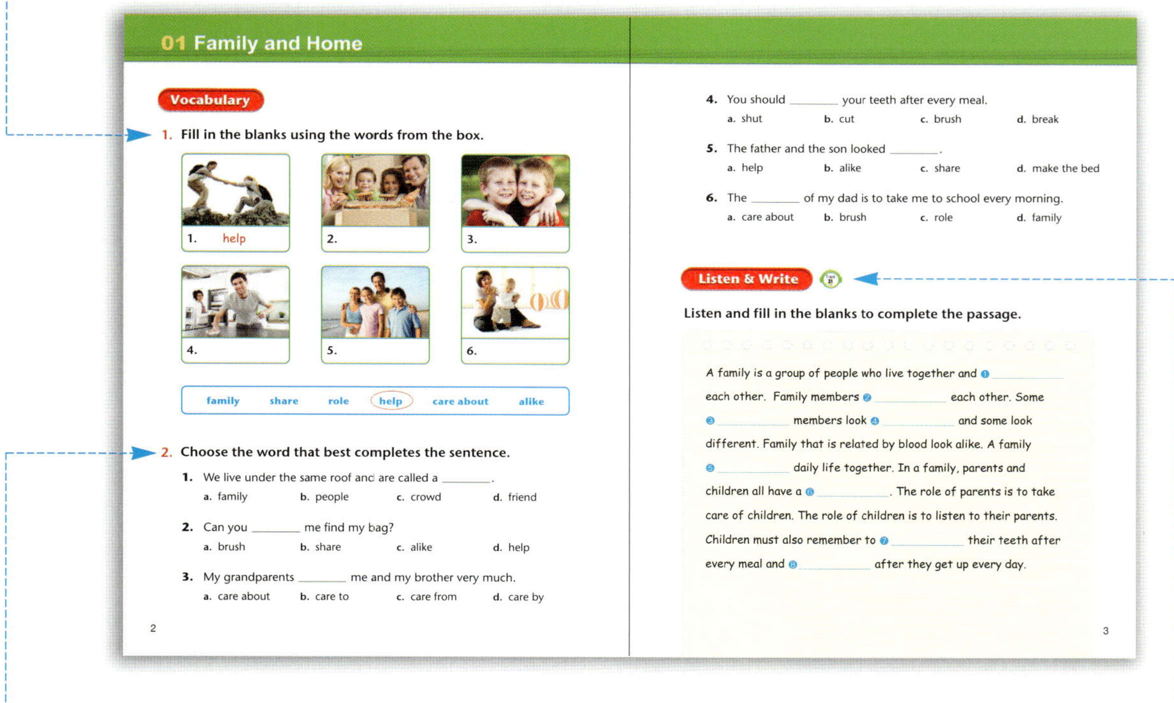

Vocabulary 2

These exercises make students use the key vocabulary words in a context that is different to that in the passage. This increases students' understanding and use of words.

Listen & Write

Students can practice their listening skills. A native speaker of English speaks the passage, and this allows students to hear the proper pronunciation of words.

Part 1
Home, School, and Neighborhood

ATR-SO1-01
MP3

family

a group of people who live together and care about each other

share

to have or use something with someone

role

the part a person plays in a group

help

to give someone assistance

care about

to give attention to someone or something

alike

in the same way

More Vocabulary

brush
to clean with something made of short hairs

make the bed
to tidy blanket or covers

help each other

care about each other

Family

alike to each other

share daily life with each other

Up Close

Daily Life of a Family

eat breakfast

learn to do things

make the bed

brush teeth

Match each word with the right picture.

1. family _______
2. share _______
3. role _______
4. help _______
5. care about _______
6. alike _______

Look at the pictures and complete the sentence.

In a family, parents and children all have a(n) _____________________ .

Match each word with its definition.

1. in the same way ______________

2. to give someone assistance ______________

3. the part a person plays in a group ______________

4. to have or use something with someone

____

5. to give attention to someone or something

____

6. a group of people who live together and care
about each other ______________

family

share

role

help

care about

alike

Circle T for true, F for false.

1. Brothers look alike.   T / F

2. People in a family do not help each other.   T / F

3. A family does not live together.   T / F

ATR-SO1-02
MP3

Read the passage. Complete the chart.

Family and Home

A family is a group of people who live together and care about each other. Family members help each other. Some family members look alike and some look different. Family that is related by blood look alike. A family shares daily life together. In a family, parents and children all have a role. The role of parents is to take care of children. The role of children is to listen to their parents. Children must also remember to brush their teeth after every meal and make the bed after they get up every day.

READING SKILL Main Idea and Details

Family members care about each other.

Family members **A**__________ each other.	Some family members look **B**__________ and some look different.	A family **C**__________ daily life together.	In a family, parents and children all have a(n) **D**__________.

Choose the correct answer.

1. The _______________ of parents is to take care of children.

    a. brush   **b.** role   **c.** share

2. A family shares _______________ together.

    a. their blood   **b.** daily life   **c.** brushing teeth

3. Children must remember to _______________.

    a. make their teeth and brush their bed

    b. brush their teeth after every meal

    c. brush their bed after they get up

4. Each family member has a role. Children _______________.

    a. take care of their parents and make their beds

    b. listen to other children and their parents listen to other parents

    c. listen to their parents and their parents take care of them

Critical Thinking

Write the correct answer.

1. How does a family usually look?

    They look _______________ to each other.

2. What does a family usually do in the kitchen in the morning?

    They _______________ together.

Key Vocabulary

ATR-SO1-03
MP3

class

a period of time to teach a group of students

classroom

a place in school used to teach a group of students

principal

the head teacher of a school

rule

an instruction about what people must do or must not do

responsibility

something that people should do

fair

in a way that is right and honest

Rules to Follow at School

Up Close

What is a school building composed of?

Match each word with the right picture.

1. class ______
2. classroom ______
3. principal ______
4. rule ______
5. responsibility ______
6. fair ______

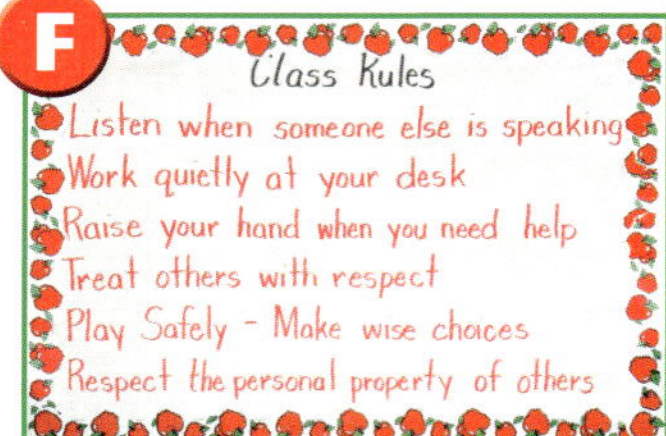

Look at the pictures and write the word that best fits in the blank.

Place

______

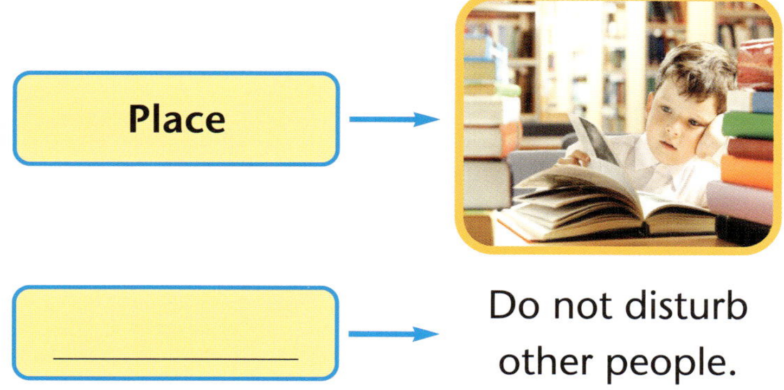

Do not disturb
other people.

Be quiet and listen
to the teacher.

Match each word with its definition.

1. in a way that is right and honest

   ____

2. something that people should do

   ____

3. the head teacher of a school _______________

4. a period of time to teach a group of students

   ____

5. a place in school used to teach a group of students _______________

6. an instruction about what people must do or must not do _______________

class
classroom
principal
rule
responsibility
fair

True or False

Circle T for true, F for false.

1. A classroom is a period of time to teach a group of students.　　T / F

2. A responsibility is something that people should do.　　T / F

3. A principal is an instruction about what people must do or must not do.　　T / F

ATR-SO1-04
MP3

Read the passage. Complete the chart.

Time for School

At school, there are some important rules to remember. In the classroom during class, we must be quiet and listen to the teacher. We must also be quiet and not disturb other people in the library. In the hallway we should walk carefully. The cafeteria also has rules we must follow when we eat our lunch. We have a responsibility to follow rules because rules help us be fair. The rules also help us be safe. The principal of the school, teachers, and students should all follow the rules to make a happier and safer school.

READING SKILL Cause and Effect

We have rules to follow.

CAUSE

We must be Ⓐ ____________ during class.

We must not disturb other people in the Ⓑ ____________ .

We should walk carefully in the Ⓒ ____________ .

EFFECT

We will be Ⓓ ____________ and safe in school.

Choose the correct answer.

1. At school, there are some rules to ______________ .

    a. make   **b.** follow   **c.** disturb

2. What rule should we follow in the hallway?

    a. listen carefully   **b.** eat carefully   **c.** walk carefully

3. In the library, students should ______________ .

    a. eat their lunch quietly and not run

    b. be quiet and not disturb others

    c. walk carefully and disturb others

4. We all have a responsibility to follow rules, ______________ .

    a. because rules help us be safe and fair

    b. but teachers and the principal do not have to

    c. but we do not have to follow rules in the classroom

Critical Thinking

Write the correct answer.

1. Name two places in a school.

____

2. Name two rules in a classroom.

____

03 Community

Key Vocabulary

ATR-SO1-05
MP3

community

a place where people live, work, and play together

neighbor

a person living near your house

address

the details of a place where you work or live

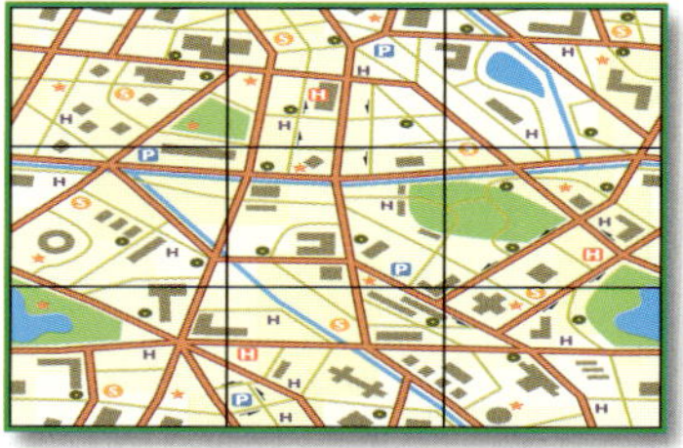

symbol

a sign, number, or letter with a certain meaning

map

a drawing of the earth's surface showing the position of things

direction

the point or position such as north, south, east, or west

More Vocabulary

map key
the words or icons showing the meanings of symbols on a map

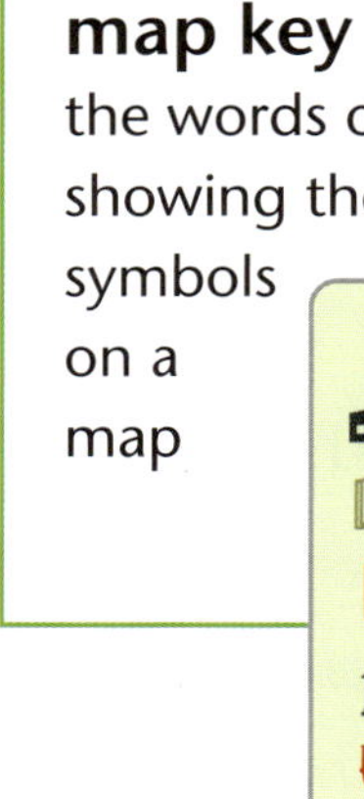

Visual Summary

Community Places

park

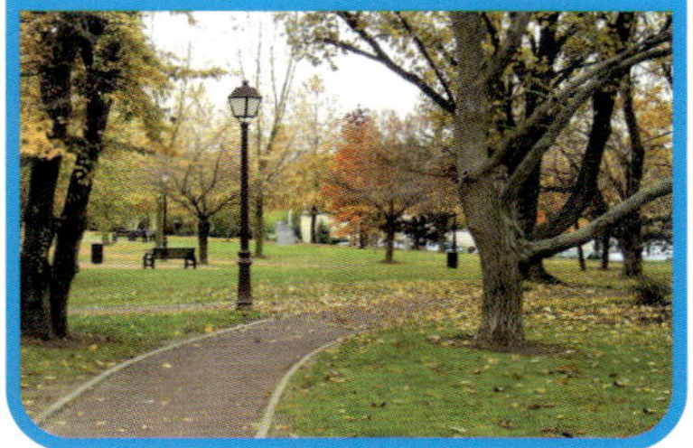

school

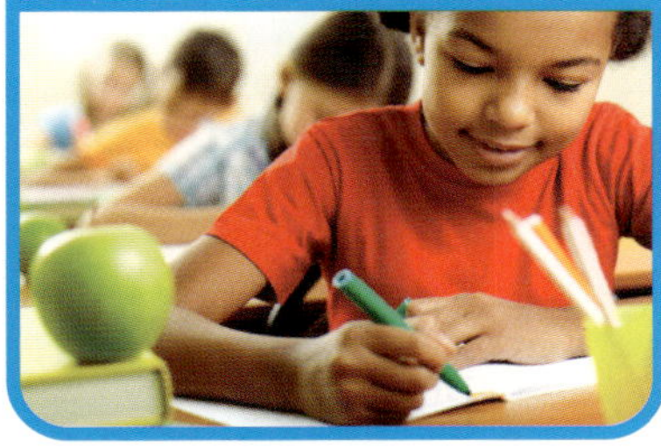

store

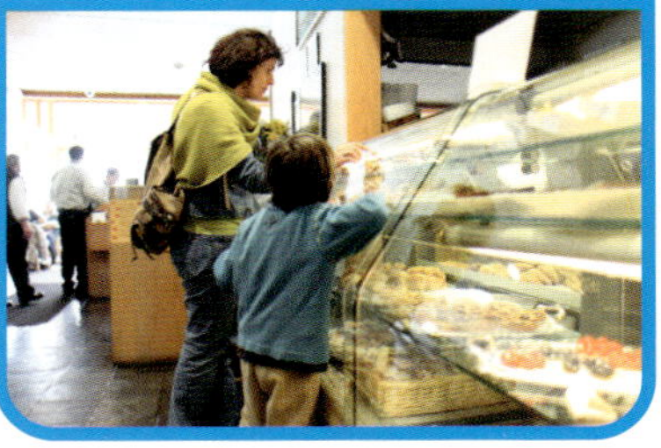

library

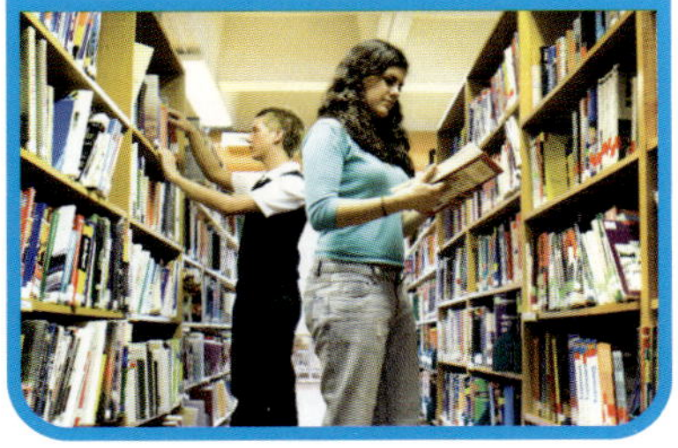

hospital

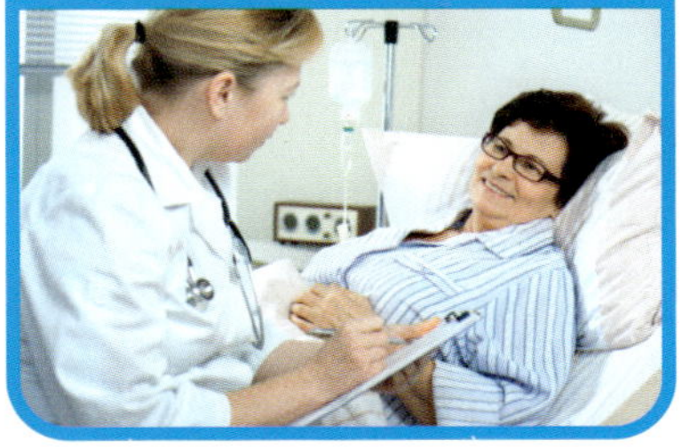

theater

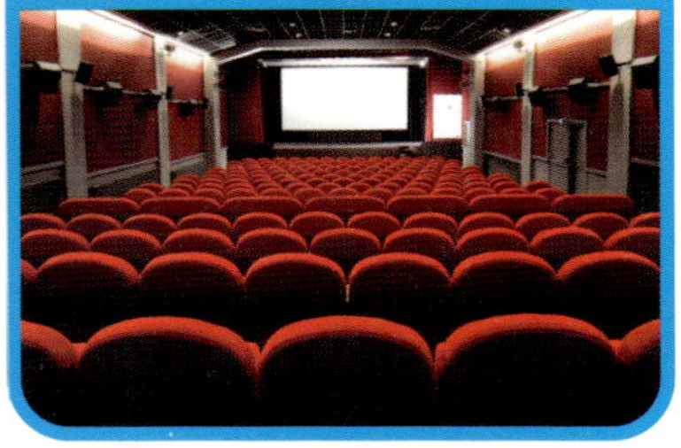

Up Close

Community Helpers

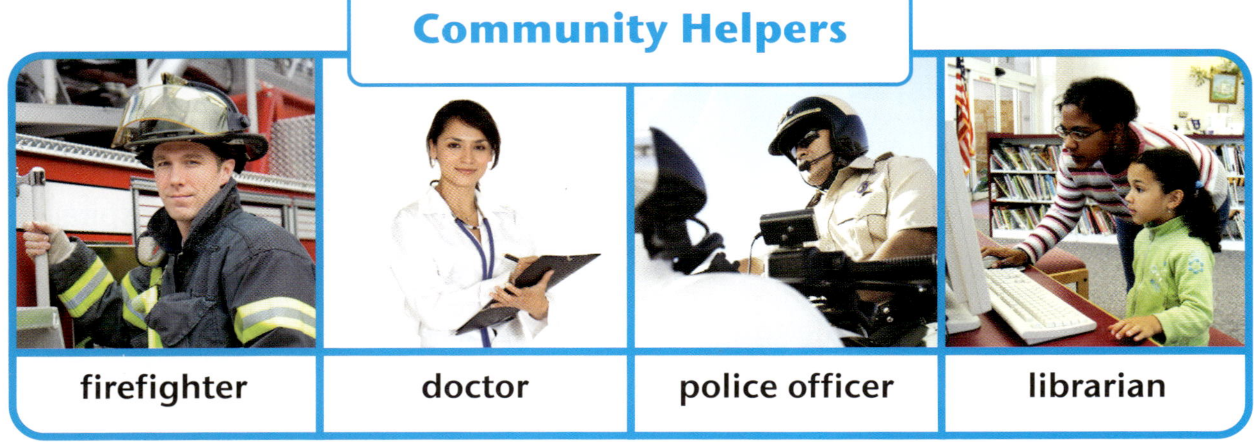

firefighter

doctor

police officer

librarian

Match each word with the right picture.

1. community _______
2. neighbor _______
3. address _______
4. symbol _______
5. map _______
6. direction _______

Look at the map and answer the question.

What is west of the school?

Match each word with its definition.

1. a place where people live, work, and play

____

2. the details of a place where you work or live

____

3. a person living near your house _______________

4. a sign, number or letter with a certain meaning

____

5. the point or position such as north, south, east, or west _______________

6. a drawing of the earth's surface showing the positions of things _______________

> community
>
> neighbor
>
> address
>
> symbol
>
> map
>
> direction

True or False

Circle T for true, F for false.

1. A map is a place where people live and work together.　　T / F

2. My neighbor is the details of the place where I live.　　T / F

3. A symbol is a sign with a certain meaning.　　T / F

Read the passage. Complete the chart.

Community

A community is a place where people live, work, and play. A community has many helpers. Some helpers keep us safe and healthy. Some helpers keep the community clean. A community has many places. A community has places like a school, hospital,

park and library. If you are looking for a place, you can ask a neighbor for help. Every place has an address to help you find the place. A map is an important tool to help you find where you want to go. To use a map, you should find the meanings of the symbols from the map key. Understanding the symbols will put you in the right direction to find your destination.

READING SKILL Classify

A community is where people live, work, and play.

A ____________

They keep us safe and **B** ____________.
They keep the community **C** ____________.

places

A community has a school, **D** ____________, park, library, etc.

Choose the correct answer.

1. Every place has a(n) _____________ to help you find it.

   a. symbol   **b.** helper   **c.** address

2. To use a map, you should understand the _____________.

   a. map symbols   **b.** north map   **c.** symbol directions

3. A community has many helpers who _____________.

   a. keep us clean and keep the community healthy

   b. keep us safe and keep the community clean

   c. make maps and understand the symbols on a map

4. If you are looking for a place, you can _____________.

   a. find the direction using a symbol in a library

   b. get a community helper to make you a map key

   c. ask a neighbor for directions or use a map

Write the correct answer.

1. Name three places in your community.

____

2. Name three community helpers.

____

Part 2
We Are Good Citizens

Key Vocabulary

citizen

a person who lives and works in a community

law

a rule that people in a community must follow

obey

to do what you are told to do

fair

equal to everyone

safe

in no danger

clean

not dirty

More Vocabulary

traffic sign
a sign that gives drivers and walkers information

break laws
to do something that laws tell us is wrong

problem
a trouble or difficulty

Why must citizens follow laws?

fair

problems

Laws

Breaking · Obeying

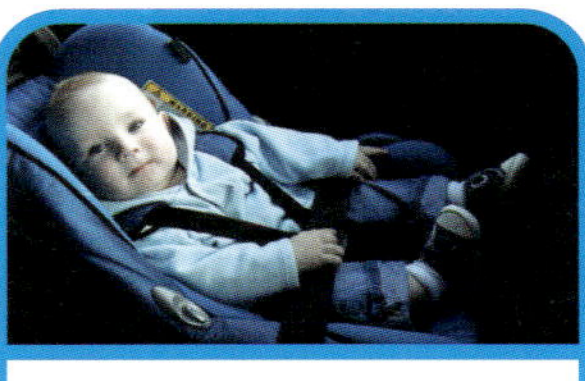

safe

clean

* There are many kinds of laws in a community.
* People can make or change laws.

Up Close

Signs that Show the Laws

| Children cross here. | Many foods should have labels. | Nobody can swim here. |

Which picture goes with each word?

1. citizen _______
2. law _______
3. obey _______
4. fair _______
5. safe _______
6. clean _______

Complete the sentence that best describes the pictures.

People in a community must _______________ laws.

Match each word with its definition.

1. not dirty ______________

2. in no danger ______________

3. equal to everyone ______________

4. to do what you are told to do ______________

5. a rule that people in a community must follow

   ____

6. a person who lives and works in a community

   ____

> citizen
>
> law
>
> obey
>
> fair
>
> safe
>
> clean

Circle T for true, F for false.

1. A citizen is a person who lives and works in a community.   **T / F**

2. Fair means equal to everyone.   **T / F**

3. If you break laws, you obey the laws.   **T / F**

Read the passage. Complete the chart.

People Need Laws

Citizens are people who live and work in a community. A community can be small like a neighborhood, and large like a city or country. So when someone lives in a neighborhood, he or she is called a neighborhood citizen. When they live in the United States of America, they are called American citizens. Every community has laws which citizens should obey or follow. Laws help keep a community clean, safe, and fair. Signs in parks say "No dumping." Traffic signs tell walkers when to cross the road, and tell drivers when to stop. Citizens can enjoy living in a fair community when everybody obeys the laws. If they don't and break laws, they make problems for a community.

READING SKILL Cause and Effect

Every community has laws.

CAUSE	EFFECT
Citizens **A**____________ or **B**____________ the laws.	Citizens can enjoy a clean, safe, and fair society.
Citizens **C**____________ the laws.	Citizens make **D**____________ for a community.

Choose the correct answer.

1. _______________ are people who live in a community.

    a. Neighborhoods   **b.** Citizens   **c.** Laws

2. Traffic signs tell drivers when _______________.

    a. to stop   **b.** to dump   **c.** to be clean

3. Every community has laws which _______________.

    a. citizens should break and not follow

    b. citizens should obey or follow

    c. citizens should make for others

4. When someone lives in a neighborhood, _______________.

    a. they are called an American citizen

    b. they are called a good citizen

    c. they are called a neighborhood citizen

Critical Thinking

Write the correct answer.

1. Obeying the law makes what kind of society?

Obeying the law makes a clean, _______________, and _______________ society.

2. What happens if people break the law?

If people break the law, it makes _______________.

ATR-SO1-09
MP3

right

something that you can do or have by law

responsibility

taking care of something and taking the blame if it goes wrong

choose

to pick something or someone from among others

respect

polite behavior toward someone

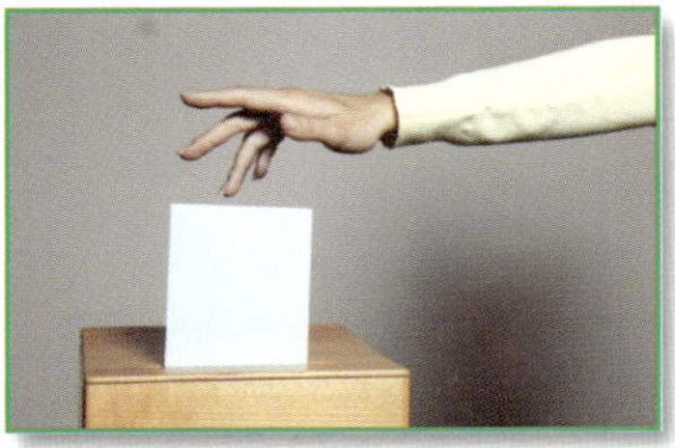

duty

something that you must do

act

to do something

More Vocabulary

express
to tell others your ideas using words, gestures or behavior

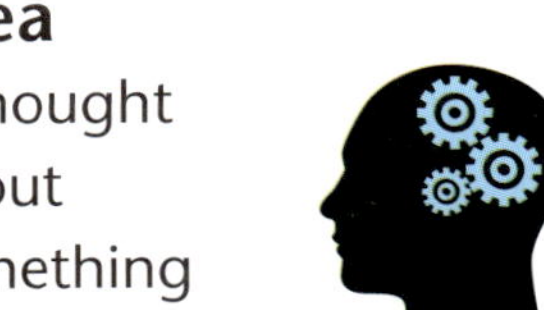

idea
a thought about something

Rights and Responsibilities

Rights	Responsibilities
 Acting freely	 Making laws
 Expressing your ideas	 Following laws
 Choosing leaders	 Showing respect for others

Up Close

How to Show Respect

listening to teachers

following rules

helping others

Which picture goes with each word?

1. right _______

2. responsibility _______

3. choose _______

4. respect _______

5. duty _______

6. act _______

Look at the pictures and write the word that best describes them.

how to show _______________________

Match each word with its definition.

1. something that you must do ____________

2. to do something ____________

3. polite behavior toward someone ____________

4. something that you can do or have by law

   ____

5. to pick something or someone from among

   others ____________

6. taking care of something and taking the blame

   if it goes wrong ____________

right

responsibility

choose

respect

duty

act

True or False

Circle T for true, F for false.

1. Responsibility is polite behavior toward someone.   T / F

2. Your duty is what you must do.   T / F

3. Right means to do something with a purpose.   T / F

Read the passage. Complete the chart.

What Can Citizens Do?

All citizens have rights and responsibilities. We have the right to express our ideas, and the right to act freely. Choosing the leaders of our community is also a right. We can do our part in making laws by choosing our leaders, so this can be one of our responsibilities too. Another important responsibility we have is to follow laws and show respect for others. These are the key duties of citizens. So remember we can enjoy our rights, but we must do our duties at the same time. In this way, we can be good citizens to make our community a better, safer, and happier place to live.

READING SKILL Cause and Effect

All citizens have rights and responsibilities.

CAUSE

We have the right to express our
Ⓐ_______________, act Ⓑ_______________, and choose our Ⓒ_______________.

We have responsibilities to follow
Ⓓ_______________, and show
Ⓔ_______________ for others.

EFFECT

We can make our community a better, safer, and happier place.

Choose the correct answer.

1. Everyone has the right to express their ______________.

    a. responsibilities   **b.** ideas   **c.** laws

2. All citizens have ______________.

    a. laws and rights

    b. responsibilities and rights

    c. duties and respect

3. We can do our part in making laws ______________.

    a. by acting freely and following others

    b. choosing our citizens

    c. by choosing our leaders

4. The key duties of citizens are to ______________.

    a. show respect for others and follow laws

    b. act freely and show respect for others

    c. choose their leaders and express their ideas

Critical Thinking

Write the correct answer.

1. Name two rights that people have.

____

2. Name two responsibilities that people have.

____

Key Vocabulary

ATR-SO1-11
MP3

leader

a person who is in charge of a group

mayor

the leader of a city or a town

vote

to make a choice

election

choosing a leader or leaders by a vote

count

to say numbers one by one and to know how many there are

adult

a person who is fully grown

More Vocabulary

ballot
a piece of paper on which you mark your vote

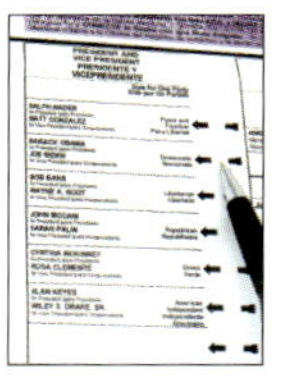

governor
the leader of a state in the United States

decision
a choice you make after thinking carefully

Process of Choosing Community Leaders

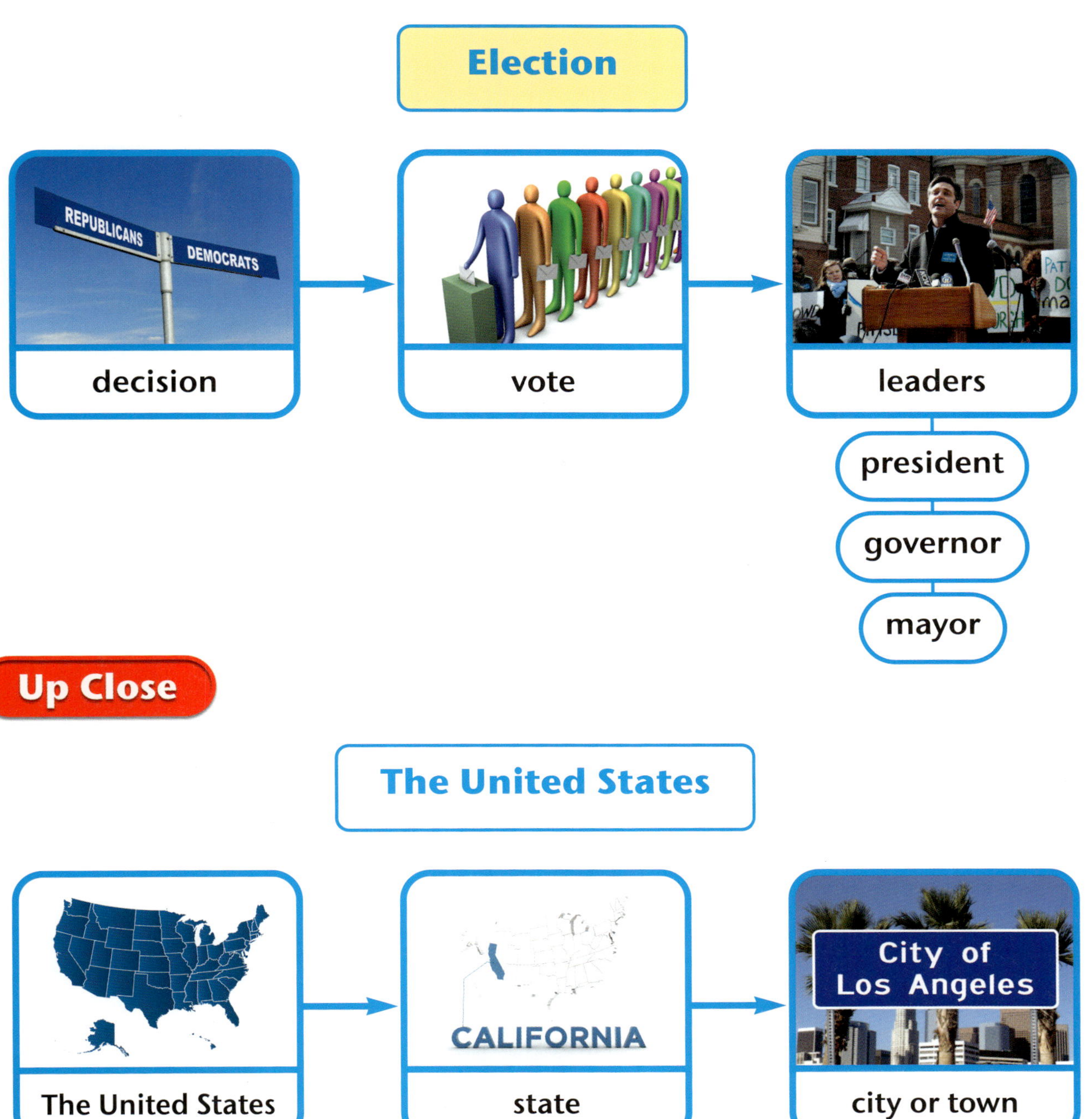

- The United States has 50 states.
- A state has many cities and towns.

Which picture goes with each word?

1. leader   ______
2. mayor   ______
3. vote   ______
4. election   ______
5. count   ______
6. adult   ______

Write the correct type of leader for each picture.

1.

______

2.
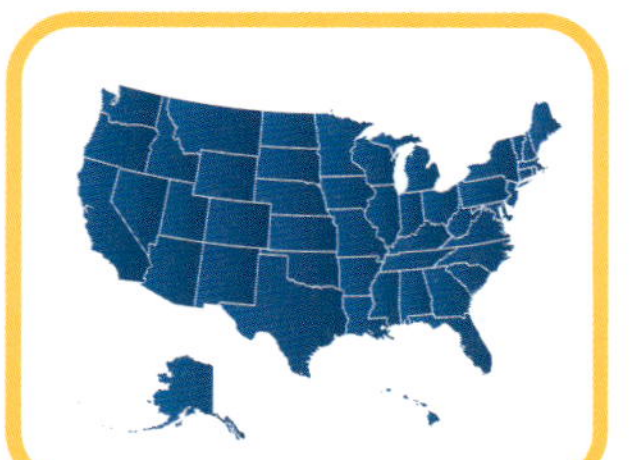

______

3.

______

Match each word with its definition.

1. a person who is in charge of a group

____

2. a person who is fully grown ______________

3. the leader of a city or a town ______________

4. to make a choice ______________

5. choosing a leader or leaders by a vote

____

6. to say numbers one by one and to know how
many there are ______________

> leader
>
> mayor
>
> vote
>
> election
>
> count
>
> adult

True or False

Circle T for true, F for false.

1. A ballot means choosing a leader or leaders by a vote.　　**T / F**

2. A mayor is the leader of a state in the United States.　　**T / F**

3. A decision means a choice you make after thinking carefully.　　**T / F**

Read the passage. Complete the chart.

Choosing Community Leaders

In communities in the United States of America, every adult can choose their leaders. This means only people 18 years or older can vote. In a town or city, people can vote for a mayor. In a state, people vote for a governor. People choose their leaders in an election. During an election they go to the voting place, and mark their decision on a ballot in the voting booth. These ballots are counted in the election and a new leader is chosen. In America, people vote for new mayors and governors every four years. The leader makes important decisions about the community. So every citizen who is an adult should not miss this chance to vote.

READING SKILL Main Idea and Details

Every adult can choose their leaders.

People vote for a(n) **A** ________ in a town or city.	People vote for a(n) **B** ________ in a state.	People choose their leaders in a(n) **C** ________.	People mark their **D** ________ on a(n) **E** ________.

Choose the correct answer.

1. Every _______________ can choose their leader.

    a. president   **b.** ballot   **c.** adult

2. In a _______________, people vote for a governor.

    a. state election   **b.** state mayor   **c.** state count

3. Ballots are counted in an election, _______________.

    a. and a new leader is named

    b. but a leader chooses the new leader

    c. and the community is chosen

4. A mayor is the leader of a town or city, _______________.

    a. and a president is the leader of a state

    b. and the mayor is elected by the president

    c. and a governor is the leader of a state

Critical Thinking

Write the correct answer.

1. What kind of person is allowed to vote?

    A(n) _______________ is allowed to vote.

2. Where do people mark their ballots?

    People mark their ballot in the voting _______________.

Part 3
Everything Changes

Key Vocabulary

ATR-SO1-13
MP3

history

the story of events that happened in earlier times

past

the time before now

present

the time now

future

the time to come after now

fact

a thing that is true and can be proven

fiction

something that is made up and not true

Everything changes over time

Past			

Present			

Up Close

Timeline

A timeline shows how things change over time.

Tom is born.

Tom's 4th birthday

Tom's first bike

Which picture goes with each word?

1. history _______
2. past _______
3. present _______
4. future _______
5. fact _______
6. fiction _______

Place each picture in the timeline.

| 1900s | 1920s | 1940s | 1960s | 1980s | 2000s |

(   )   (   ) (   )

a.

b.

c.

Match each word with its definition.

1. the time now _______________

2. the time before now _______________

3. the time to come after now _______________

4. a thing that is true and can be proven

   ____

5. something that is made up and not true

   ____

6. the story of events that happened in earlier times

   ____

> history
>
> past
>
> present
>
> future
>
> fact
>
> fiction

True or False

Circle T for true, F for false.

1. We live in the past.   **T / F**

2. Fiction is a thing that is true and can be proven.   **T / F**

3. A timeline shows what happened in time.   **T / F**

ATR-SO1-14
MP3

Read the passage. Complete the chart.

Things Change with Time

Everything changes from the past to the future. The story of events that happened in the past is called history. History is not fiction. History shows us how things change. The past is different from the present. In the

past, you were smaller. In the present, you are getting bigger. The city you live in also changes. In the past, your city was small and not many people lived there. In the present, your city is bigger and there are more people. If we want to see changes in history, we can use a timeline. A timeline can help us to understand when things happened. Our history is full of facts telling us what, when, and where things happened.

READING SKILL Compare and Contrast

Past	Present
You were smaller.	You are getting **Ⓐ**______________.
Your city was small, not many people lived there.	Your city is bigger. There are **Ⓑ**______________ people.
Everything changes from the **Ⓒ**______________ to the **Ⓓ**______________.	

Choose the correct answer.

1. The past is different from the _____________.
   a. fiction   b. present   c. history

2. A timeline can show what happened in _____________.
   a. the past   b. the present   c. the future

3. The story of events that happened in the past _____________.
   a. is called a timeline, and it is fiction
   b. is called the future, and it is fiction
   c. is called history, and it is fact

4. To see changes in history, you can use a timeline _____________.
   a. which shows when things happened
   b. which shows why things happened
   c. which shows fiction, not facts

Critical Thinking

Write the correct answer.

1. In the past you were smaller, but now you are bigger.

   Everything _____________________.

2. What are facts about people, places, and events called?

   ____

08 Changes in Family Life

ATR-SO1-15
MP3

life
the way a person lives

dress
a type of clothing for women and girls

shelter
a place to live or stay

clothing
coverings that people wear

crop
a plant that people grow as food

farm
a piece of land where people grow crops or animals

More Vocabulary

harvest
the gathering of the crops

corn
a kind of plant with yellow seeds, which is used for food

wheat
a kind of plant with grains that flour is made from

What has changed in family life?

	Clothing	Shelter	Food
Past	dress	farm house	harvesting by hand
Present	t-shirt & jeans	city house	harvesting by machine

Up Close

Different and the Same

In the past, women worked at home. Today, both women and men have jobs outside the home.

Some of the games children played in the past have stayed the same.

Which picture goes with each word?

1. life _______
2. dress _______
3. shelter _______
4. clothing _______
5. crop _______
6. farm _______

A

B

C

D

E

F

Review 2

Look at the pictures. Fill in the blank to complete the sentence.

The way people live has _____________________ .

Match each word with its definition.

1. a place to live or stay _______________

2. the way a person lives _______________

3. coverings that people wear _______________

4. a plant that people grow as food _______________

5. a piece of land where people grow crops or animals _______________

6. a type of clothing for women and girls _______________

> life
>
> dress
>
> shelter
>
> clothing
>
> crop
>
> farm

True or False

Circle T for true, F for false.

1. A shelter is a covering that people wear.　　T / F

2. A farm is the gathering of the crops.　　T / F

3. Flour is made from wheat.　　T / F

Read the passage. Complete the chart.

Changes in Family Life

Life in the past was harder for people. The way people live now has changed but some things are also similar. People in the past and now need food, shelter, and clothing. Corn and wheat are kinds of crops. At harvest time, these crops are gathered. In the past, on farms, people harvested crops using their hands. Now, people have machines to help them and the work has become easier. Shelter has also changed. In the past, people lived in small houses. Now people also live in apartments. Our clothing has changed. Women in the past wore dresses only. Women today wear many different kinds of colorful and interesting clothes.

READING SKILL Compare and Contrast

Past	Present
Harvested crops using hands.	Harvest crops using machines, so work has become **A**______________.
People lived in small houses.	People live in **B**______________.
Women wore dresses **C**______________.	Women wear many colorful and interesting clothes.
People need food, **D**______________, and **E**______________.	

Choose the correct answer.

1. _______________ is something that people wear on their bodies.

   a. Shelter **b.** Clothing **c.** Flour

2. Crops are gathered at _______________.

   a. an apartment **b.** a shelter **c.** harvest time

3. Crops like corn and wheat _______________.

   a. are grown on farms and are gathered

   b. can only be gathered by hand, not by machines

   c. are grown in shelters and are gathered

4. In the past, people lived in small houses, _______________.

   a. and now they only live in farm houses

   b. and now they also live in apartments

   c. but people no longer need to live in shelters

Critical Thinking

Write the correct answer.

1. In the past, people harvested crops by hand. How do they harvest crops now?

   People harvest crops _______________.

2. How are the lives of women today different from the lives of women in the past?

   Today, they have jobs _______________.

Key Vocabulary

invention

something new or a new way of doing something

tool

a thing that helps people do a job

education

teaching or training people and the things people learn

information

facts or details that you know about something

communication

the way people share ideas and exchange information

machine

a tool with complex parts that is used for a particular job

More Vocabulary

printing press
a machine that is used to make books or newspapers

slate
a writing tablet

Communication Inventions

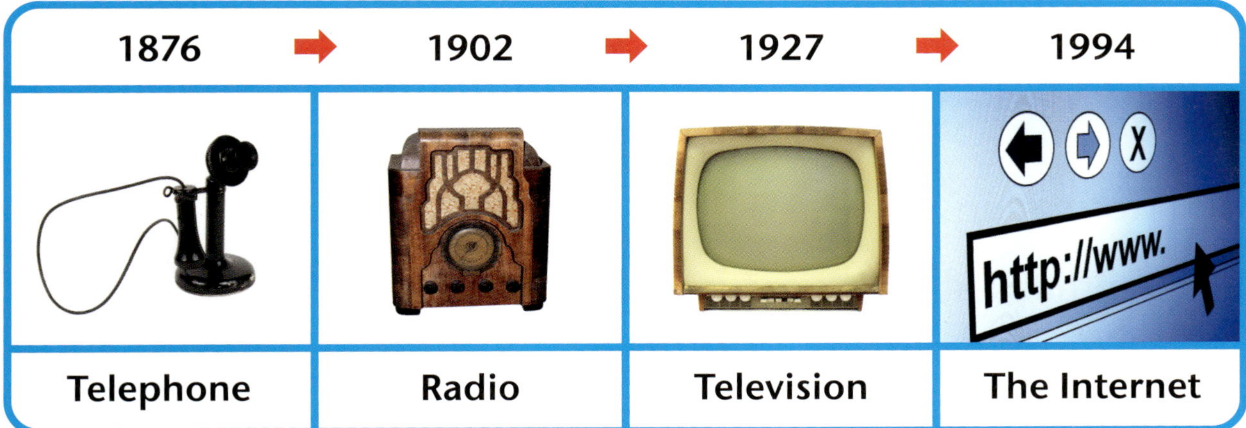

Up Close

Inventions in Making Books

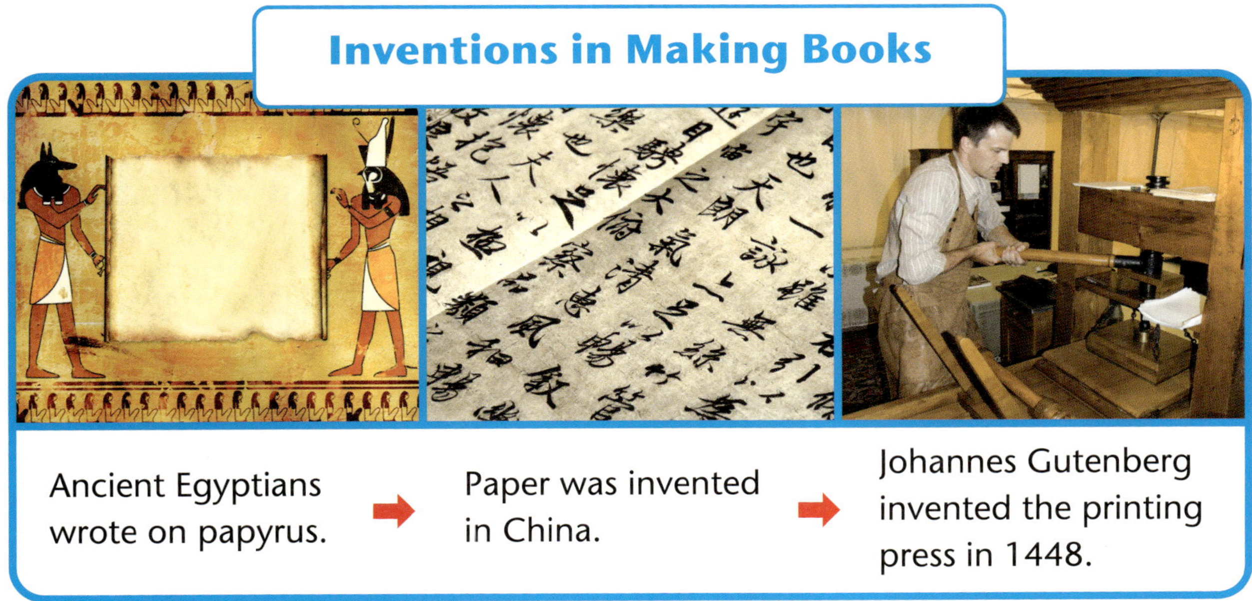

Ancient Egyptians wrote on papyrus.

Paper was invented in China.

Johannes Gutenberg invented the printing press in 1448.

Which picture goes with each word?

1. invention ______
2. tool ______
3. education ______
4. information ______
5. communication ______
6. machine ______

Review 2

Look at the pictures and write the word that best describes them.

____

Match each word with its definition.

1. a thing that helps people do a job

   ____

2. facts or details that you know about something ______________

3. something new or a new way of doing something ______________

4. the way people share ideas and exchange information ______________

5. teaching or training people and the things people learn ______________

6. a tool with complex parts that is used for a particular job ______________

invention

tool

education

information

communication

machine

True or False

Circle T for true, F for false.

1. Inventions are facts or details that you know about something.   T / F

2. Paper was invented in Egypt.   T / F

3. A printing press is a machine that is used to make books or newspapers.   T / F

ATR-SO1-18
MP3

Read the passage. Complete the chart.

Changes in Communication

People use tools to communicate. New inventions make communication easier. People in the past used slates, chalk, and ink for writing. In the present, people use computers and notebooks for writing. The telephone and printing press are inventions that help communication. In the present, people use cellular phones to talk. The printing press is a machine that makes newspapers and books. In the past people got information by talking to other people. Now newspapers and books are important for people to learn from. Modern communication tools such as the Internet are important to our daily life and education. Every day we use new inventions and important tools to help us communicate.

READING SKILL Compare and Contrast

Past	Present
People used slates, chalk, and Ⓐ_____________ for writing.	People use Ⓑ_____________ and notebooks for writing.
People got information by talking to other people.	People get information from newspapers and Ⓒ_____________. People use Ⓓ_____________ to talk.
People use tools to Ⓔ_____________.	

Choose the correct answer.

1. Inventions have made ______________ easier.

    a. telephones   **b.** newspapers   **c.** communication

2. What is the most modern communication tool?

    a. a slate   **b.** the Internet   **c.** a printing press

3. The printing press is ______________.

    a. a tool used to make movies and newspapers

    b. a machine that makes newspapers and books

    c. a communication tool that makes notebooks

4. The cellular phone and printing press ______________.

    a. are inventions that help us communicate

    b. were invented by Johannes Gutenberg

    c. are machines that we use for writing

Critical Thinking

Write the correct answer.

1. Name three communication inventions you use today.

____

2. What was used to write on before paper?

____

Part 4
People Work

ATR-SO1-19
MP3

Key Vocabulary

needs

things that you must have to live

wants

things that you don't need but wish to have

scarcity

not enough of something

money

something that people use as a means of exchange

bill

paper money

coin

money that is made of metal

More Vocabulary

quarter

a coin that is worth 25 cents

penny

a coin that is worth 1 cent

Needs and Wants

Up Close

We use money to buy what we need and want.

But we do not always have enough money.

This is called scarcity.

We have to make choices about what to buy.

Which picture goes with each word?

1. needs   _______
2. wants   _______
3. scarcity   _______
4. money   _______
5. bill   _______
6. coin   _______

Choose the correct answer.

1. 

  a. needs
  b. wants

2. 

  a. needs
  b. wants

3. 

  a. needs
  b. wants

Match each word with its definition.

1. paper money ______________

2. not enough of something ______________

3. money that is made of metal ______________

4. things that you must have to live ______________

5. things that you don't need but wish to have

   ____

6. something that people use as a means of

   exchange ______________

> needs
>
> wants
>
> scarcity
>
> money
>
> bill
>
> coin

True or False

Circle T for true, F for false.

1. Scarcity means there is enough of something.   T / F

2. We need to make choices about what to buy.   T / F

3. Wants are things that you must have to live.   T / F

Read the passage. Complete the chart.

Needs and Wants

People have needs and wants. Needs are things we must have to live. Food, shelter, and clothes are needs. Wants are things we would like to have. Dolls and candy are wants. We use money to buy what we need and want. There are different types of money. Bills and coins are types of money. A bill has more value than a coin. A coin is money made of metal. There are many types of coin. A quarter and a penny are two kinds of coin in America.
Sometimes there is not much of something. This is called a scarcity. We do not always have enough money to buy all we want. That's why we have to choose between things.

READING SKILL Compare and Contrast

Needs	Ⓐ_____________
things we Ⓑ_____________ have to live	things we would like to have
Ⓒ_____________, shelter, and clothes	things like dolls and candy
We use Ⓓ_____________ to buy what we need and want.	

Choose the correct answer.

1. What does a bill have more value than?

    a. scarcity   **b.** metal   **c.** coin

2. Food, ______________ are all needs.

    a. clothes, and candy   **b.** shelter, and clothes   **c.** toys, and candy

3. A penny and a quarter are ______________.

    a. two kinds of coin in America

    b. types of candy sold in America

    c. both bills which are used in America

4. What happens when there is a scarcity of something?

    a. We have enough money to buy all the things that we want.

    b. There is not much of something and we might not be able to buy it.

    c. We only have enough money to buy the things we want, not need.

Critical Thinking

Write the correct answer.

1. Name two wants.

____

2. Why do we make choices about what to buy?

We do not always have ______________________ ______________________.

11 Goods and Services

ATR-SO1-21
MP3

goods

things that people buy or use

service

work that people do for others

price

the amount of money that you have to give to buy something

sell

to give something for money

buy

to get something by giving money for it

trade

to give someone one thing and get another thing from them

More Vocabulary

pay
to give money for something

grow
to raise plants or animals

compare
to see how things are different or similar

Goods
Home
Car
Book
Food
People meet their wants and needs.
Services
Mail carrier
Bus driver
Doctor
Hairstylist

Up Close

Money
Goods or Services
Buyer
Seller

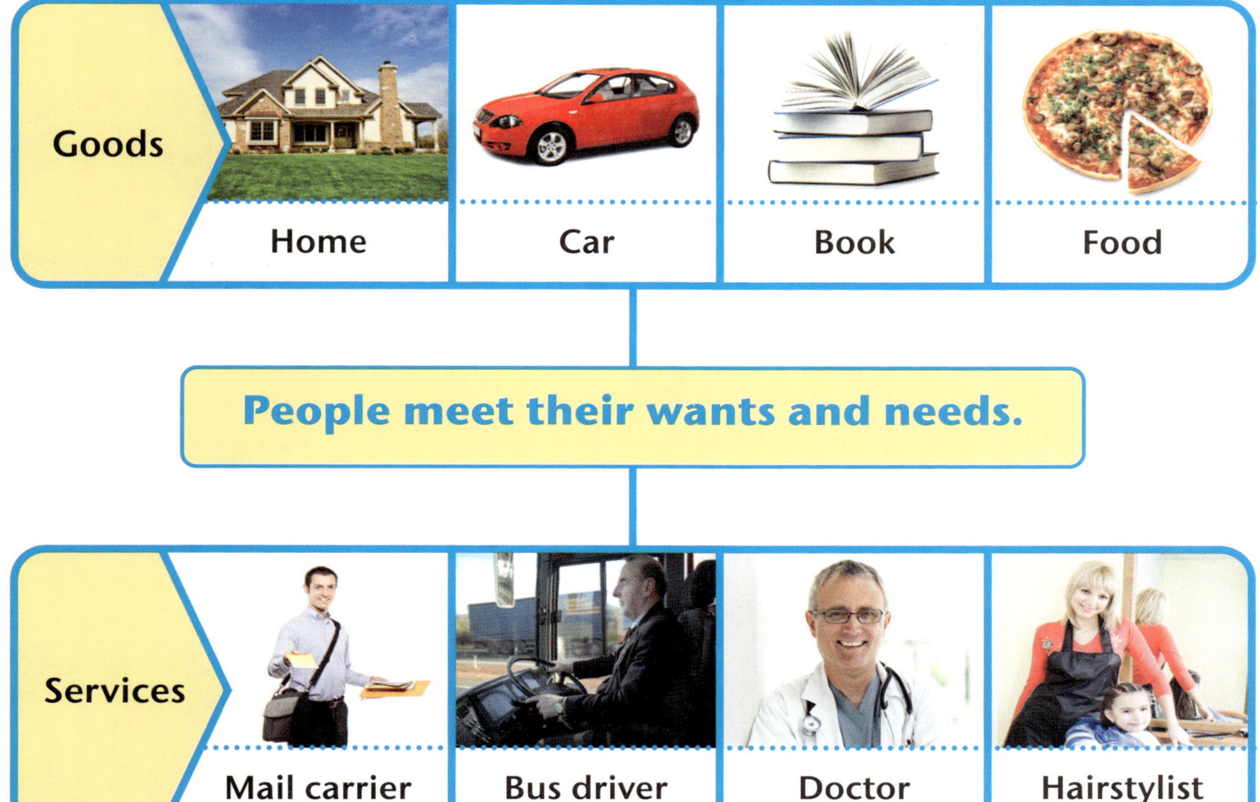

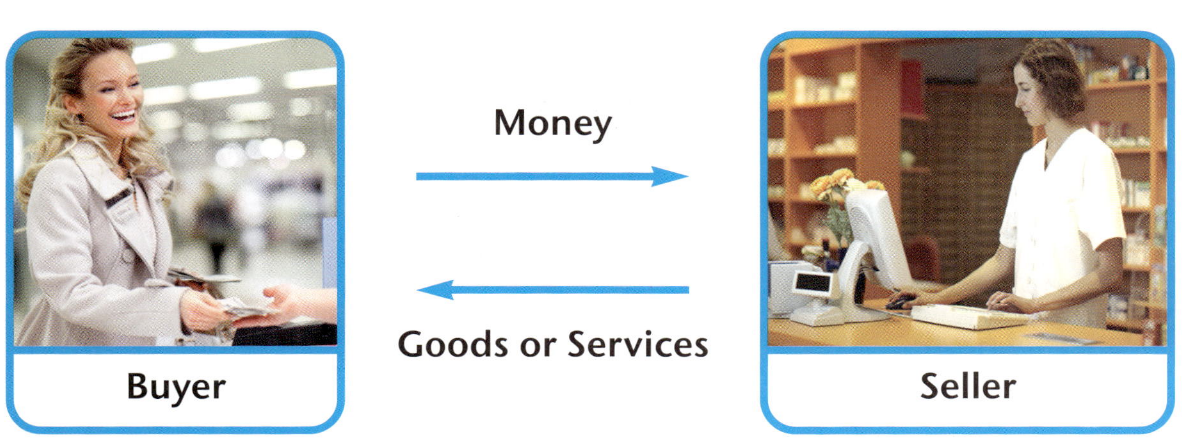

Which picture goes with each word?

1. goods _______

2. service _______

3. price _______

4. sell _______

5. buy _______

6. trade _______

Choose the correct answer for each picture.

1.

a. goods
b. services

2.

a. goods
b. services

3.

a. goods
b. services

Match each word with its definition.

1. to give something for money _____________

2. to get something by giving money for it

____

3. things that people buy or use _____________

4. work that people do for others _____________

5. to give someone one thing and get another

thing from them _____________

6. the amount of money that you have to give to

buy something _____________

> **goods**
>
> **service**
>
> **price**
>
> **sell**
>
> **buy**
>
> **trade**

True or False

Circle T for true, F for false.

1. Trade means to see how things are different or similar. **T / F**

2. A service is a type of work people do for others. **T / F**

3. Sellers pay money for goods or services. **T / F**

Read the passage. Complete the chart.

ATR-SO1-22
MP3

Goods and Services

People buy goods and services to meet their wants and needs. Bread, apples, cars, and toys are all goods. You get services when you take a bus, go to a hairstylist, or see a doctor. People make or grow goods and sell them in stores. They sell services too. They sometimes come to you with their services. A mail carrier delivers your letters to you. You have to pay money to buy goods and services. When you do this, you should compare the prices and quality. You can also trade goods or services. Children at times trade their lunch or small chores with each other.

READING SKILL Compare and Contrast

Goods	Services
People Ⓐ____________ or grow goods and Ⓑ____________ them in stores. Bread, apples, cars, and toys are goods.	You get services when you take a bus, go to a hairstylist, or see a doctor.
People buy goods and services to meet their Ⓒ____________ and Ⓓ____________. You have to Ⓔ____________ money to buy goods and services.	

Choose the correct answer.

1. What does a mail carrier deliver to you?

    a. money   **b.** letters   **c.** chores

2. People buy _____________ to meet their needs and wants.

    a. lunch and chores

    b. doctors and mail carriers

    c. goods and services

3. When you buy a good or service, you _____________.

    a. can only buy them from a store

    b. should compare the quality and prices

    c. have to trade a good or service for it

4. Some people make or grow goods to sell, and _____________.

    a. others sell services that people want or need

    b. those people sell those goods only to mail carriers

    c. these goods are all called services

Critical Thinking

Write the correct answer.

1. What do buyers do to get goods or services?

____

2. How can people get things without buying them?

____

Spending and Saving

Key Vocabulary

ATR-SO1-23
MP3

spend

to give money to someone else to get goods or services

save

not to spend money and keep it for later

cost

the amount of money that you have to pay to get or do something

item

one thing that is part of a list or set

grocery

a store where you can buy food or other goods

bank

a safe place where you can save or borrow money

More Vocabulary

shopping list

a list of things that you need to buy

piggy bank

a pig-shaped money box that children save coins in

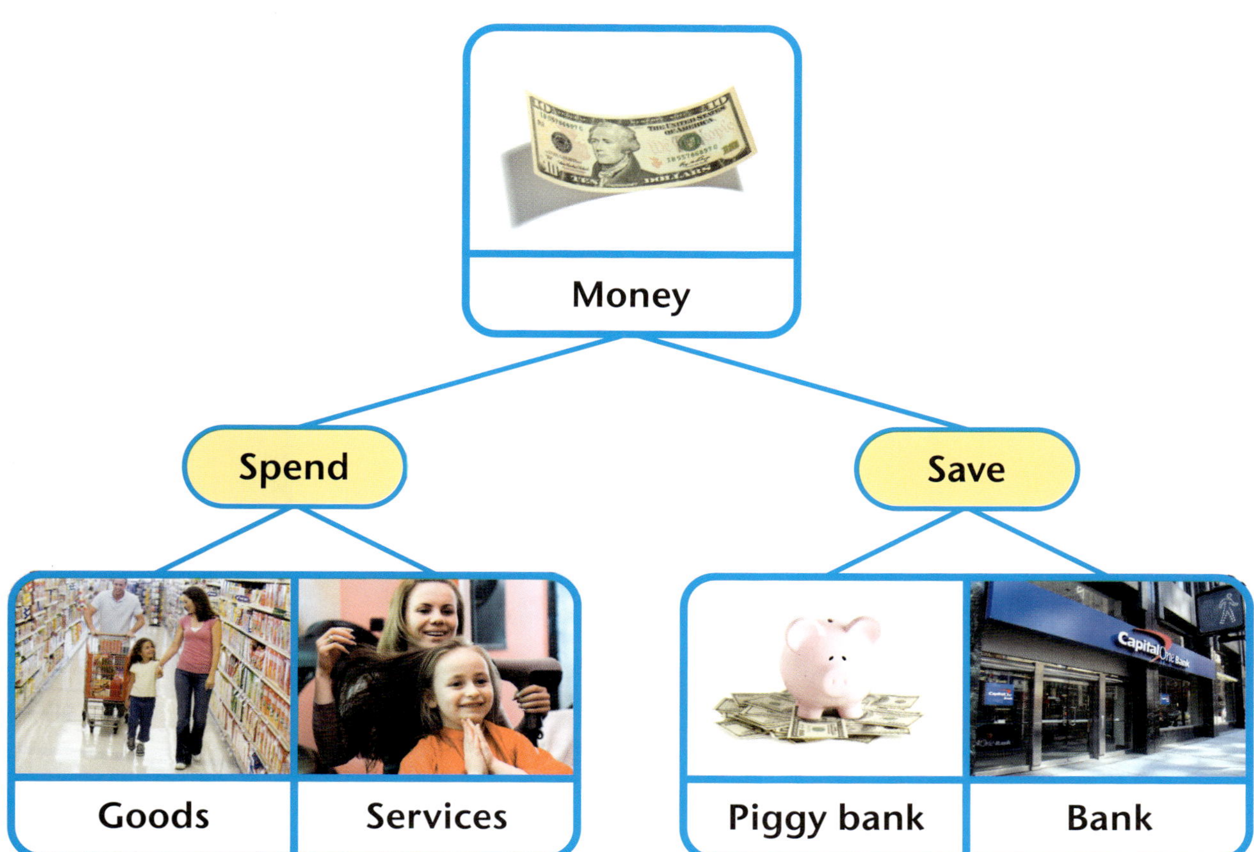

Up Close

Making Choices

You can't buy everything you want. If you want to buy things, you should make choices by looking at the cost of things.

Which picture goes with each word?

1. spend _______
2. save _______
3. cost _______
4. item _______
5. grocery _______
6. bank _______

Complete the sentence that best describes the pictures.

We should make _______________ about how to spend money.

Match each word with its definition.

1. one thing that is part of a list or set

   ____

2. not to spend money and keep it for later

   ____

3. a store where you can buy food or other goods

   ____

4. a safe place where you can save or borrow

   money _______________

5. the amount of money that you have to pay to

   get or do something _______________

6. to give money to someone else to get goods or

   services _______________

> spend
>
> save
>
> cost
>
> item
>
> grocery
>
> bank

True or False

Circle T for true, F for false.

1. If you save money, you get goods from someone else. **T / F**

2. A grocery is a list of things. **T / F**

3. A bank is a store where you can buy food. **T / F**

ATR-SO1-24
MP3

Read the passage. Complete the chart.

Spending and Saving

Spending and saving money is fun to learn about. If you want to buy food and other items, you must spend money. But before you go to a grocery store, you should make a shopping list. Write all the items you need or want to buy. Then think if you really need or want them. You should make choices about what to buy, because you do not always have enough money. You should choose goods after you look at their cost. People spend money, and people also save money. Your parents save their money in a bank. You can save your money in a piggy bank. You can save money to use later.

READING SKILL Classify

Spend Money	Save Money
You should make a **Ⓐ** _____________ before you spend money. You should choose goods after you look at their **Ⓑ** _____________ .	Your parents save their money in a **Ⓒ** _____________ . You can save money to use **Ⓓ** _____________ .

Choose the correct answer.

1. What do you need to spend if you want to buy something?

    a. bank   **b.** money   **c.** goods

2. Many people _____________ money.

    a. spend and save   **b.** buy and sell   **c.** choose and sell

3. You should look at a good's cost, _____________.

    a. but you do not need a shopping list

    b. and then choose if you should buy it

    c. and then sell it in a grocery store

4. Your parents can save their money in a bank, _____________.

    a. and you can save yours in a piggy bank

    b. and you can save yours by buying things

    c. and you can save yours in a grocery store

Write the correct answer.

1. What should you do before you buy something?

    Make a(n) _____________________.

2. What kind of things can we spend money on?

____

Part 5
Where We Live

Earth

the third planet from the Sun

globe

a round object that is a model of Earth

land

the hard surface of Earth

continent

a very large area of land

ocean

a large area of salt water that covers most of Earth

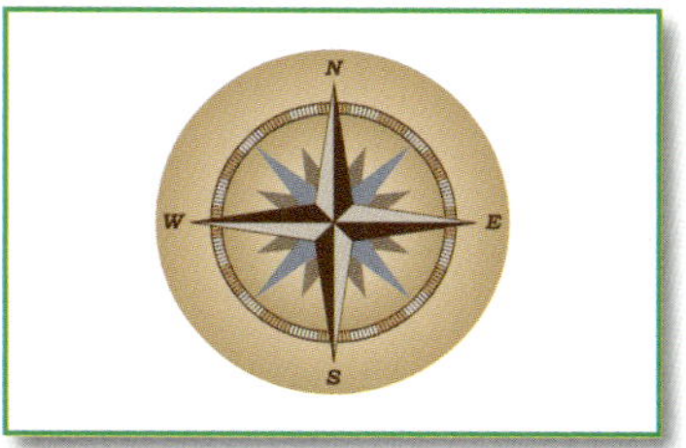

compass rose

a symbol that shows directions on maps

The World

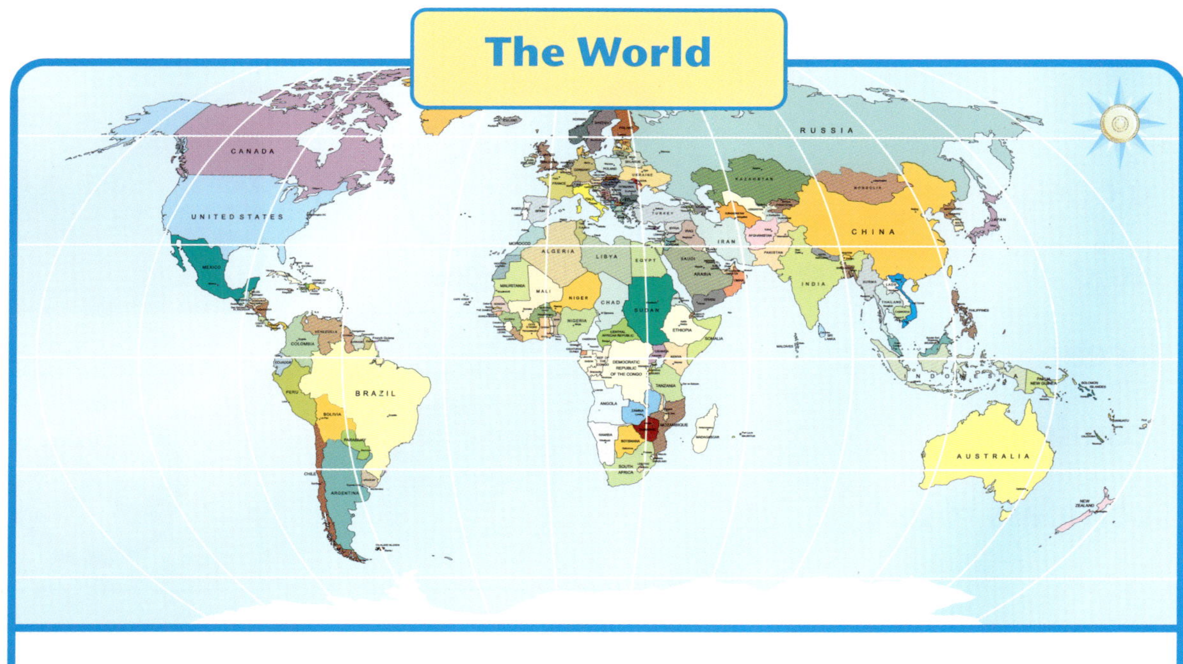

* A map is flat but a globe is round just like Earth.
* They both show Earth's land and water.

Earth's Land and Water

Continents		Oceans
Africa	Europe	Arctic Ocean
Antarctica	North America	Atlantic Ocean
Asia	South America	Indian Ocean
Australia		Pacific Ocean

Which picture goes with each word?

1. Earth _______

2. globe _______

3. land _______

4. ocean _______

5. continent _______

6. compass rose _______

A 

B 

C 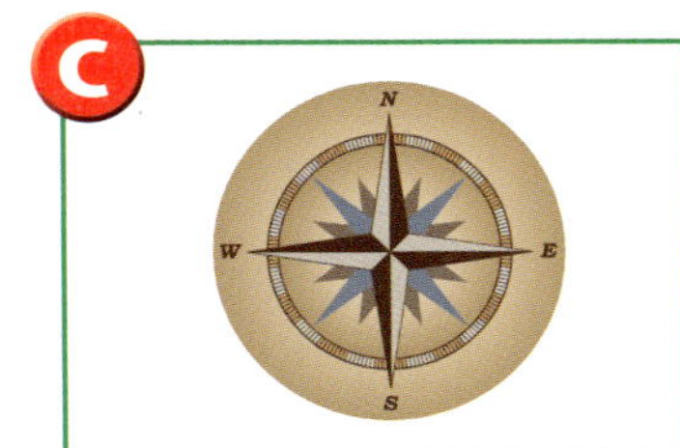

D 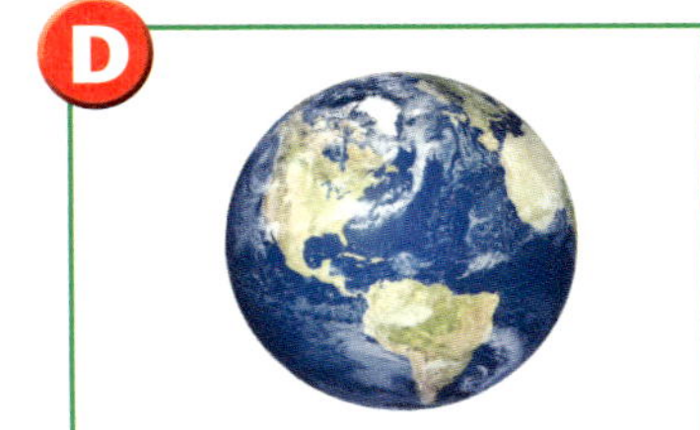

E 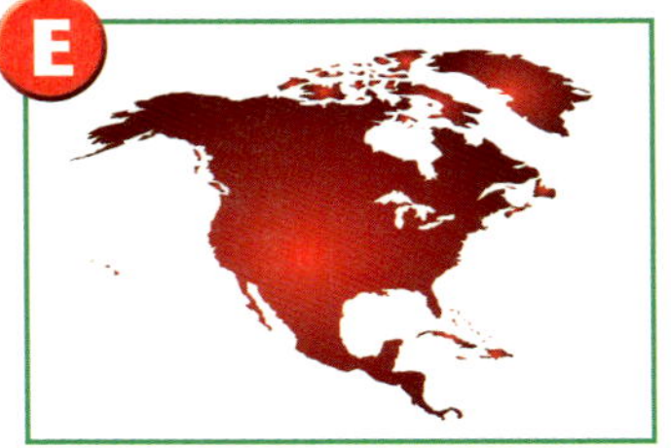

F 

Complete the sentences that best describe the pictures.

A map is ______________ but a globe is ______________ just like Earth.

They both show Earth's ______________ and ______________.

Match each word with its definition.

1. a large area of salt water that covers most of Earth ________________

2. the third planet from the Sun ________________

3. a round object that is a model of Earth ________________

4. a symbol that shows directions on maps ________________

5. the hard surface of Earth ________________

6. a very large area of land ________________

> Earth
>
> globe
>
> land
>
> ocean
>
> continent
>
> compass rose

Circle T for true, F for false.

1. A globe is a flat object that is a model of Earth.   **T / F**

2. An ocean is a very large area of land.   **T / F**

3. A compass rose is a symbol that shows directions on maps.   **T / F**

Read the passage. Complete the chart.

ATR-SO1-26
MP3

Here on Earth

The planet where we live is called Earth. It is made up of air, water, and land. A very large area of land is called a continent. North America is a continent where most people speak English. On Earth, there is more water than land. An ocean is a large body of salt water. If the Earth is so big, how can we find new places? A compass rose, globe, and map are things we can use to discover places on the Earth. We can use a globe to plan our trip. Then we should use a compass rose and a map to find our direction. Take a look at a globe, try and plan a trip to a fun new continent.

READING SKILL Main Idea and Details

Earth is made up of air, water, and land.

A large area of land is called a(n) **A**________.

A(n) **B**________ is a large body of salt water.

A compass rose, **C**________, and map are things to discover places on the Earth with.

Choose the correct answer.

1. What is a very large area of land called?

    a. continent   **b.** ocean   **c.** globe

2. Earth is made up of water, _____________.

    a. and salt water   **b.** land and air   **c.** continents and compasses

3. North America is a continent where _____________.

    a. most people speak English

    b. most people live in the ocean

    c. most people uses compass roses

4. What are things we can use to plan a trip to another continent?

    a. We can use an ocean, which is a large body of salt water.

    b. We can use a globe, but should not use a map.

    c. We can use a map, compass rose, and a globe.

Critical Thinking

Write the correct answer.

1. Explain how maps and globes are different.

____

2. Explain how maps and globes are the same.

____

14 Weather and Seasons

Key Vocabulary

weather

the conditions of the air outside

season

any of the four main periods of the year

spring

the season between winter and summer

summer

the warmest season of the year, coming after spring

fall

the season between summer and winter

winter

the coldest season of the year, coming after fall

More Vocabulary

temperature
a measure of how hot or cold something is

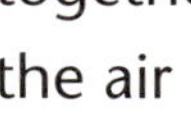

cloud
many drops of water together in the air

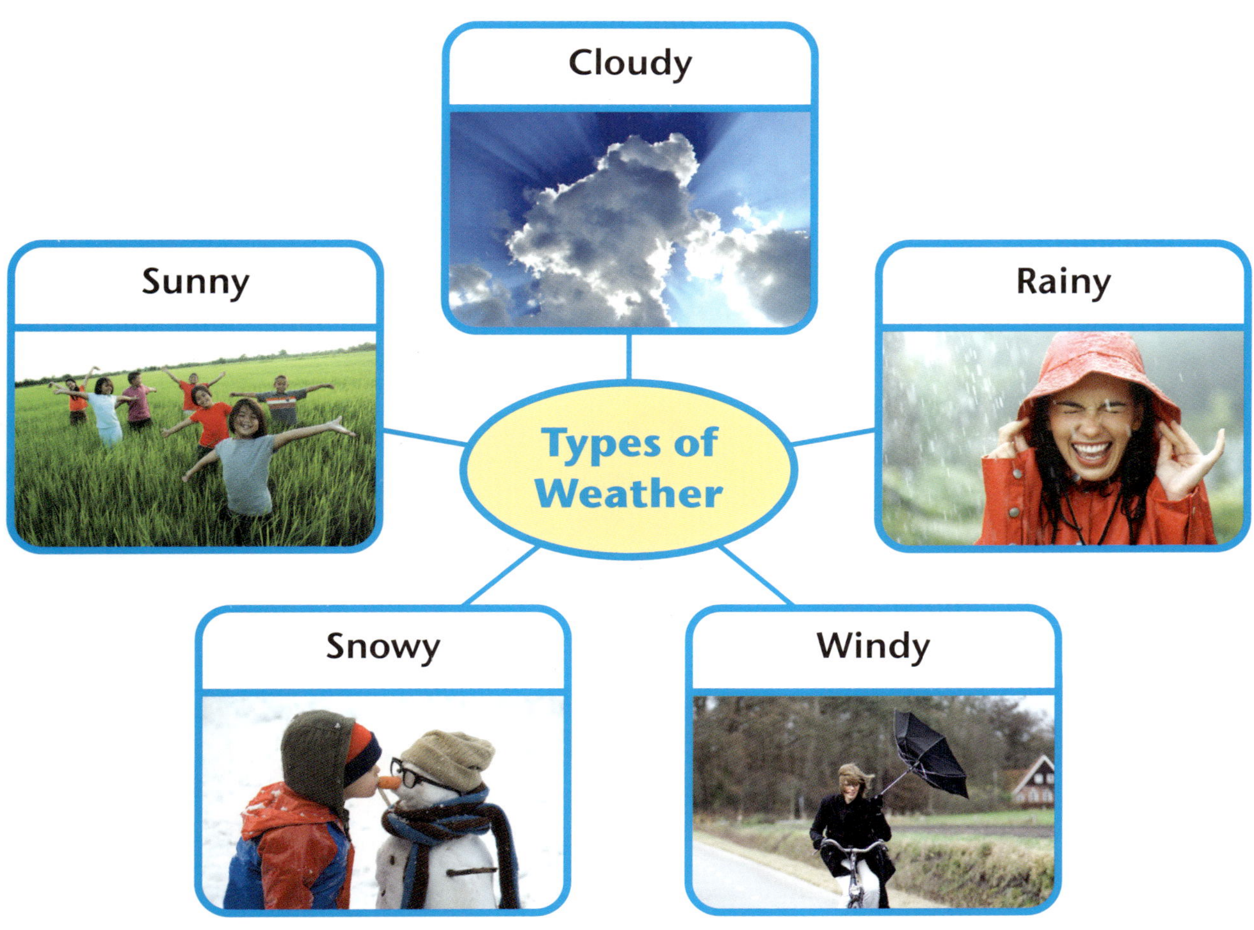

Up Close

How Weather Affects Us

Sunny	Snowy	Rainy
We can plant lots of flowers.	We can play in the snow.	We should put on a raincoat.

Which picture goes with each word?

1. weather ______
2. season ______
3. spring ______
4. summer ______
5. fall ______
6. winter ______

Review 2

Complete the sentence to best describe the pictures.

We dress and play in a way that is best for the ______________ outside.

Match each word with its definition.

1. any of the four main periods of the year

____

2. the conditions of the air outside _______________

3. the coldest season of the year, coming after fall

____

4. the warmest season of the year, coming after

spring _______________

5. the season between summer and winter

____

6. the season between winter and summer

____

weather

season

spring

summer

fall

winter

True or False

Circle T for true, F for false.

1. Weather is how hot or cold something is. **T / F**

2. Cloud is the many drops of water together in the air. **T / F**

3. Winter is the coldest season of the year. **T / F**

Read the passage. Complete the chart.

Weather and Seasons

We have four seasons every year. Every season has different weather. The weather affects how we dress and how we live. In winter, the temperature is very low. The weather is cold and we need to dress warm in scarves and gloves. In spring, the weather is warmer. Animals come out of their homes and flowers bloom. In summer, the weather is very hot and there is a lot of daylight. In summer, there are a lot of clouds. Dark clouds mean rain. In summer, people enjoy playing outside and swimming in the ocean. In fall, the weather is cooler and leaves fall from the trees. In fall, people and animals prepare for the cold winter.

READING SKILL Main Idea and Details

The weather affects how we dress and how we play.

| In winter, the **A**________ is very low. We need to dress warm. | In spring, animals come out and flowers **B**________. | In summer, the weather is very **C**________. People enjoy swimming in the ocean. | In fall, the weather is cooler and **D**________ fall from the trees. |

Choose the correct answer.

1. What changes with the change of seasons?

    a. spring   **b.** weather   **c.** beaches

2. In winter, the _______________.

    a. temperature is low   **b.** weather is hot   **c.** animals wear gloves

3. In summer, there are a lot of clouds _______________.

    a. which mean it is very cold

    b. which means it could rain

    c. which means that flowers will bloom

4. In fall, the weather is cooler and _______________.

    a. people and animals prepare for the cold winter

    b. trees and animals begin to fall as it is going to snow

    c. people start to go to the beach to swim

Critical Thinking

Write the correct answer.

1. In what season do people go to the beach?

____

2. In what season do you need gloves and a scarf?

____

15 Land and Water

ATR-SO1-29
MP3

mountain

the highest type of land

plain

a large flat piece of land

desert

a very dry area of land

river

a large stream of moving water

valley

the low land between mountains
and hills

lake

a large area of fresh water

hill

a higher
area of land

island

a piece of land with
water all
around it

Up Close

Two Kinds of Water on Earth

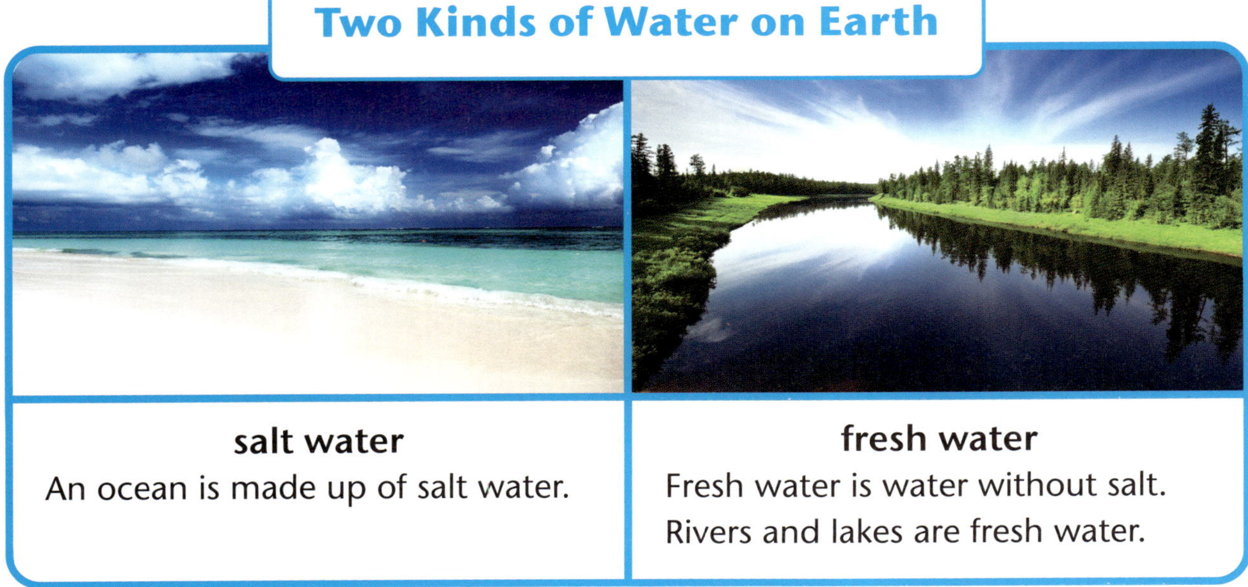

Which picture goes with each word?

1. mountain ______
2. plain ______
3. desert ______
4. river ______
5. valley ______
6. lake ______

Complete the sentence to best describe the pictures.

The Earth has different kinds of ______ and water.

Match each word with its definition.

1. a very dry area of land _______________

2. the highest type of land _______________

3. a large flat piece of land _______________

4. a large area of fresh water _______________

5. a large stream of moving water _______________

6. the low land between mountains and hills

   ____

> mountain
>
> plain
>
> desert
>
> river
>
> valley
>
> lake

True or False

Circle T for true, F for false.

1. A lake is smaller than an ocean.   T / F

2. Lakes and rivers are salt water.   T / F

3. A hill is a piece of land with water all around it.   T / F

Read the passage. Complete the chart.

Land and Water

There are many different types of land and water. A **mountain** is the highest kind of land. A **hill** is also high but it is smaller than a mountain. There are low **valleys** between mountains and hills. **Rivers** flow toward the ocean. They sometimes go through flat **plains** . We can grow many kinds of food on plains whether they are high or low. We cannot grow food in a dry **desert** . A **lake** , another area of water, has land all around it, so it doesn't flow to the ocean like a river. An **island** is the opposite of a lake. It is an area of land with water all around.

READING SKILL Classify

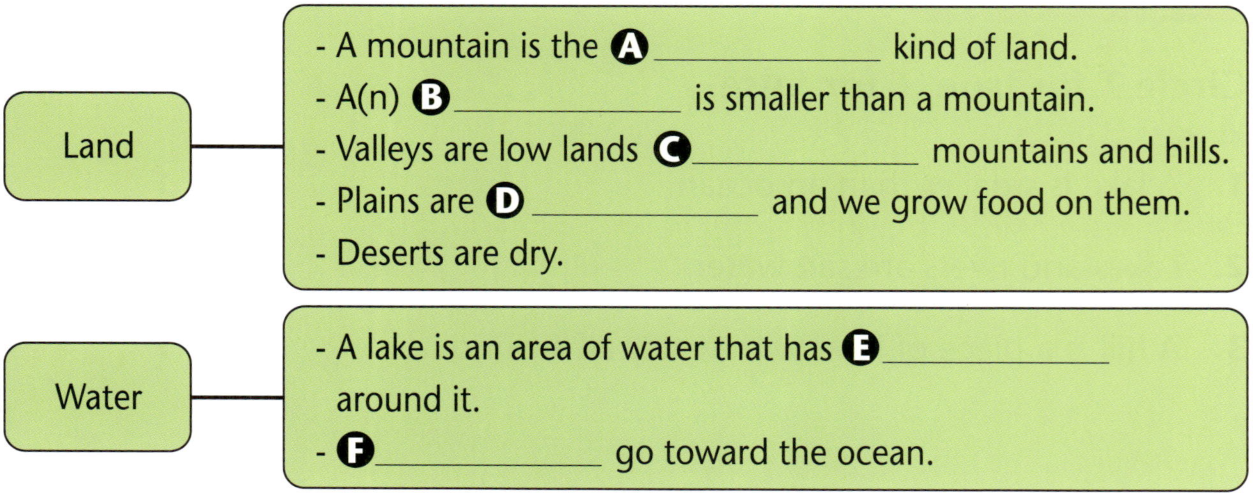

Land	- A mountain is the **A** _______________ kind of land. - A(n) **B** _______________ is smaller than a mountain. - Valleys are low lands **C** _______________ mountains and hills. - Plains are **D** _______________ and we grow food on them. - Deserts are dry.
Water	- A lake is an area of water that has **E** _______________ around it. - **F** _______________ go toward the ocean.

Choose the correct answer.

1. What is a place where we can grow food?

    a. desert   **b.** plain   **c.** rivers

2. On Earth, there are valleys between ______________.

    a. deserts and hills   **b.** rivers and beaches   **c.** hills and mountains

3. An island is not the same as a lake because ______________.

    a. an island is like a river, it flows

    b. an island has land all around it

    c. an island has water all around it

4. Rivers sometimes go through plains, ______________.

    a. and they flow up hills and mountains

    b. and they flow toward the ocean

    c. and we grow food and plants in rivers

Critical Thinking

Write the correct answer.

1. What types of high lands does Earth have?

____

2. What is the name for a small body of water surrounded by land?

____

American Textbook Reading

Social Studies 1

Workbook

American Textbook Reading

Social Studies ①

Workbook

01 Family and Home

1. Fill in the blanks using the words from the box.

1.   help

2.

3.

4.

5.

6.

family	share	role	help	care about	alike

2. Choose the word that best completes the sentence.

1. We live under the same roof and are called a __________.

   a. family   **b.** people   **c.** crowd   **d.** friend

2. Can you __________ me find my bag?

   a. brush   **b.** share   **c.** alike   **d.** help

3. My grandparents __________ me and my brother very much.

   a. care about   **b.** care to   **c.** care from   **d.** care by

4. You should __________ your teeth after every meal.

   a. shut   **b.** cut   **c.** brush   **d.** break

5. The father and the son looked __________.

   a. help   **b.** alike   **c.** share   **d.** make the bed

6. The __________ of my dad is to take me to school every morning.

   a. care about   **b.** brush   **c.** role   **d.** family

Listen & Write

ATR-SO1-W31
MP3

Listen and fill in the blanks to complete the passage.

A family is a group of people who live together and ❶ ____________ each other. Family members ❷ ____________ each other. Some ❸ ____________ members look ❹ ____________ and some look different. Family that is related by blood look alike. A family ❺ ____________ daily life together. In a family, parents and children all have a ❻ ____________. The role of parents is to take care of children. The role of children is to listen to their parents. Children must also remember to ❼ ____________ their teeth after every meal and ❽ ____________ after they get up every day.

Vocabulary

1. **Fill in the blanks using the words from the box.**

1.

2.

3.

4.

5.

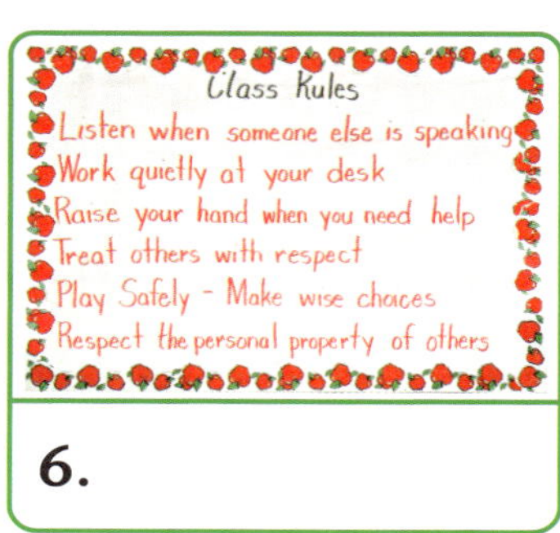

6.

class	classroom	principal	rule	responsibility	fair

2. **Choose the word that best completes the sentence.**

1. People in cars should follow every __________ of the road to be safe.

   a. principle   b. rule   c. classroom   d. playground

2. The teacher works hard during __________ to teach students.

   a. class   b. principle   c. hallway   d. follow

3. The __________ teacher treated the students equally.

   a. responsibility   b. rule   c. principal   d. fair

4. We have _________ to obey the rules.

    a. playground   **b.** principal   **c.** responsibility   **d.** class

5. At school and in the classroom, everyone should _________ the rules.

    a. follow   **b.** class   **c.** playground   **d.** rule

6. The _________ leads the whole school.

    a. playground   **b.** principal   **c.** follow   **d.** responsibility

Listen & Write

ATR-SO1-W32
MP3

Listen and fill in the blanks to complete the passage.

At school, there are some important ❶ _____________ to remember.
In the ❷ _____________ during ❸ _____________, we must be quiet
and listen to the teacher. We must also be quiet and not disturb
other people in the library. In the hallway we should walk carefully.
The cafeteria also has rules we must ❹ _____________ when we eat
our lunch. We have a responsibility to follow rules because rules
help us be ❺ _____________. The rules also help us be safe. The
❻ _____________ of the school, teachers, and students should all
follow the rules to make a happier and safer school.

Vocabulary

1. **Fill in the blanks using the words from the box.**

1. ___________

2. ___________

3. ___________

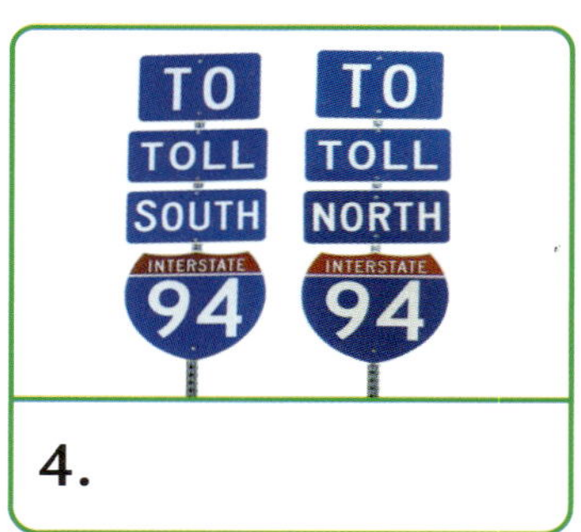

4. ___________

5. ___________

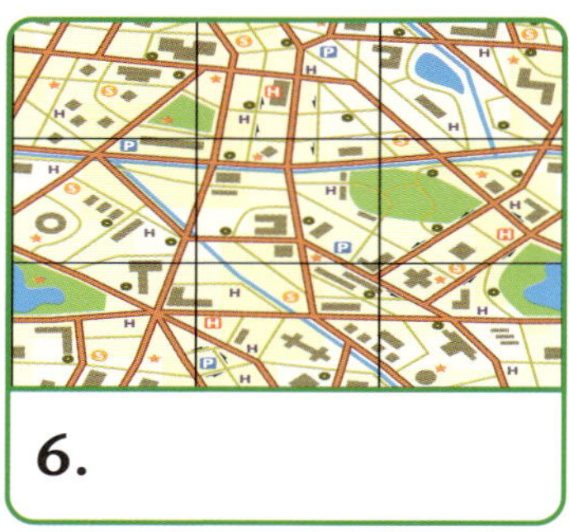

6. ___________

community   neighbor   address   symbol   map   direction

2. **Choose the word that best completes the sentence.**

1. Looking at a ___________ can help us find where we want to go.

   a. community   b. post office   c. map   d. neighbor

2. Every ___________ on a map means something about the land.

   a. direction   b. symbol   c. community   d. neighbor

3. My ___________ is very thoughtful and never makes too much noise.

   a. community   b. direction   c. map   d. neighbor

4. A good ___________ is a place where people who live together are caring to each other.

    a. community   **b.** map   **c.** address   **d.** symbol

5. I want to know the right ___________ to the post office.

    a. direction   **b.** neighbor   **c.** neighbor   **d.** map key

6. The ___________ of my house is, 263 Pine Hill Road, Dunners Town, USA.

    a. address   **b.** map key   **c.** community   **d.** symbol

Listen & Write

ATR-SO1-W33
MP3

Listen and fill in the blanks to complete the passage.

A ❶ _____________ is a place where people live, work, and play. A community has many helpers. Some helpers keep us safe and healthy. Some helpers keep the community clean. A community has many places. A community has places like a school, hospital, park and library. If you are looking for a place, you can ask a ❷ _____________ for help. Every place has an ❸ _____________ to help you find the place. A ❹ _____________ is an important tool to help you find where you want to go. To use a map, you should find the meanings of the ❺ _____________ from the ❻ _____________. Understanding the symbols will put you in the right ❼ _____________ to find your destination.

04 People Need Laws

Vocabulary

1. Fill in the blanks using the words from the box.

1.

2.

3.

4.

5.

6.

| citizen | law | obey | fair | safe | clean |

2. Choose the word that best completes the sentence.

1. __________ are people who live and work together in the same community.

   a. Citizens   b. Obey   c. Fair   d. Law

2. The __________ is a set of rules for society.

   a. safe   b. law   c. fair   d. citizens

3. Everybody must __________ the rules of their group.

   a. law   b. safe   c. clean   d. obey

4. Police officers help us and keep us __________.

    a. safe   **b.** citizens   **c.** clean   **d.** obey

5. A teacher must be __________ to everyone in their class.

    a. obey   **b.** fair   **c.** safe   **d.** clean

6. It is important to always wear __________ socks on your feet.

    a. clean   **b.** safe   **c.** law   **d.** citizens

Listen & Write

ATR-SO1-W34
MP3

Listen and fill in the blanks to complete the passage.

① __________ are people who live and work in a community. A community can be small like a neighborhood, and large like a city or country. So when someone lives in a neighborhood, he or she is called a neighborhood citizen. When they live in the United States of America, they are called American citizens. Every community has ② __________ which citizens should ③ __________ or follow. Laws help keep a community ④ __________, ⑤ __________, and ⑥ __________. Signs in parks say "No dumping." Traffic ⑦ __________ tell walkers when to cross the road, and tell drivers when to stop. Citizens can enjoy living in a fair community when everybody obeys the laws. If they don't and break ⑧ __________, they make ⑨ __________ for a community.

Vocabulary

1. **Fill in the blanks using the words from the box.**

1.

2.

3.

4.

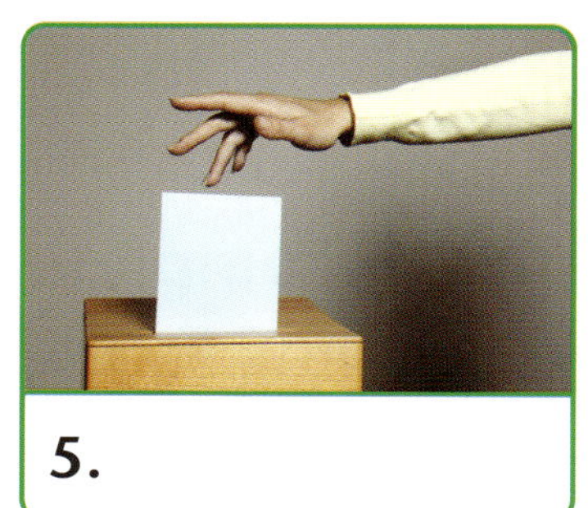

5.

6.

right	responsibility	choose	respect	duty	act

2. **Choose the word that best completes the sentence.**

1. Every person has a __________ to enjoy a happy and healthy life.

a. responsibility   b. choose   c. right   d. respect

2. We will __________ a pet to buy.

a. act   b. respect   c. duty   d. choose

3. It is the __________ of a teacher to teach students and lead the class.

a. duty   b. respect   c. act   d. choose

4. We should __________ our grandparents and always be kind to them.

   a. choose   **b.** right   **c.** respect   **d.** responsibility

5. Every person has a __________ to be a good citizen.

   a. right   **b.** responsibility   **c.** choose   **d.** respect

6. It is a good __________ to always be careful when crossing the road.

   a. idea   **b.** right   **c.** act   **d.** choose

Listen & Write

ATR-SO1-W35
MP3

Listen and fill in the blanks to complete the passage.

All citizens have ❶ ______________ and ❷ ______________ . We have the
right to ❸ ______________ our ❹ ______________ , and the right to
❺ ______________ freely. ❻ ______________ the leaders of our
community is also a right. We can do our part in making laws by
choosing our leaders, so this can be one of our responsibilities too.
Another important responsibility we have is to follow laws and show
❼ ______________ for others. These are the key ❽ ______________ of
citizens. So remember we can enjoy our rights, but we must do our
duties at the same time. In this way, we can be good citizens to
make our community a better, safer, and happier place to live.

Vocabulary

1. **Fill in the blanks using the words from the box.**

1.

2.

3.

4.

5.

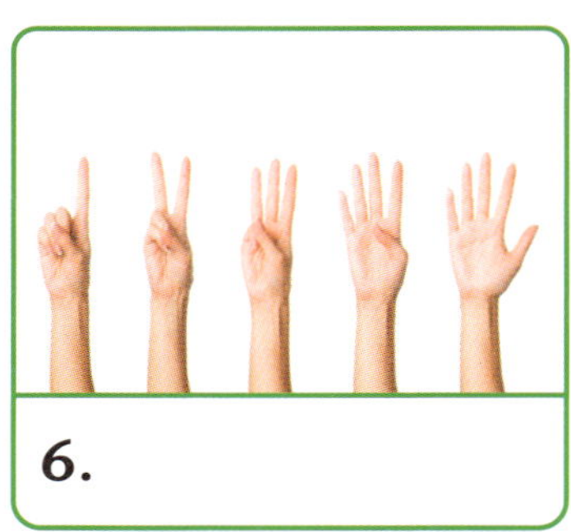

6.

| leader | mayor | vote | election | count | adult |

2. **Choose the word that best completes the sentence.**

1. The mayor is the __________ of a town.

   a. vote   **b.** leader   **c.** count   **d.** election

2. A(n) __________ is the leader of a state in America.

   a. adult   **b.** ballot   **c.** decision   **d.** governor

3. Every year, we __________ for "The Student of the Year."

   a. election   **b.** adult   **c.** vote   **d.** mayor

4. I am a child and my mom is a(n) _________.

   a. adult   **b.** mayor   **c.** leader   **d.** count

5. Before going into the toy store, we should _________ how much money we have.

   a. adult   **b.** vote   **c.** count   **d.** mayor

6. The national _________ is to choose our new leaders. It is every four years.

   a. election   **b.** governor   **c.** ballot   **d.** leader

Listen & Write

ATR-SO1-W36
MP3

Listen and fill in the blanks to complete the passage.

In communities in the United States of America, every adult can choose their ❶ _____________. This means only people 18 years or older can ❷ _____________. In a town or city, people can vote for a ❸ _____________. In a state, people vote for a ❹ _____________. People choose their leaders in an election. During an election they go to the voting place, and mark their ❺ _____________ on a ❻ _____________ in the voting booth. These ballots are ❼ _____________ in the election and a new leader is chosen. In America, people vote for new mayors and governors every four years. The leader makes important decisions about the community. So every citizen who is an ❽ _____________ should not miss this chance to vote.

07 Things Change with Time

Vocabulary

1. Fill in the blanks using the words from the box.

1.

2.

3.

4.

5.

6.

history	past	present	future	fact	fiction

2. Choose the word that best completes the sentence.

1. The time that we live in now is called the __________.

    a. timeline   **b.** present   **c.** past   **d.** future

2. The story of our past is called __________.

    a. fiction   **b.** timeline   **c.** fact   **d.** history

3. __________ books tell amazing stories that are not real.

    a. Future   **b.** Past   **c.** Fiction   **d.** Fact

4. Nonfiction books contain _________ .

    a. facts   **b.** timeline   **c.** fiction   **d.** future

5. A _________ shows you when things in the past happened.

    a. present   **b.** future   **c.** past   **d.** timeline

6. You should study hard for your _________ .

    a. timeline   **b.** fact   **c.** future   **d.** past

Listen & Write

ATR-SO1-W37
MP3

Listen and fill in the blanks to complete the passage.

Everything changes from the ❶ _____________ to the ❷ _____________ .
The story of events that happened in the past is called
❸ _____________ . History is not ❹ _____________ . History shows us
how things change. The past is different from the ❺ _____________ .
In the past, you were smaller. In the present, you are getting bigger.
The city you live in also changes. In the past, your city was small and
not many people lived there. In the present, your city is bigger and
there are more people. If we want to see changes in history, we can
use a timeline. A timeline can help us to understand when things
happened. Our history is full of ❻ _____________ telling us what,
when, and where things happened.

Vocabulary

1. Fill in the blanks using the words from the box.

1.

2.

3.

4.

5.

6.

| life | dress | shelter | clothing | crop | farm |

2. Choose the word that best completes the sentence.

1. The __________ we wear changes with each season.

   a. life   **b.** dress   **c.** clothing   **d.** farm

2. The cereal I eat every morning is made from __________.

   a. dress   **b.** corn   **c.** clothing   **d.** shelter

3. In Asian countries, rice is the most important __________.

   a. clothing   **b.** crop   **c.** farm   **d.** life

4. A _________ is a place where animals and crops are grown for selling to the market.

    a. farm   **b.** corn   **c.** wheat   **d.** shelter

5. _________ time is when farm people must work extra hard.

    a. Farm   **b.** Corn   **c.** Life   **d.** Harvest

6. Each Sunday, the little girl likes to wear her favorite _________ to church.

    a. life   **b.** harvest   **c.** dress   **d.** shelter

Listen & Write

ATR-SO1-W38
MP3

Listen and fill in the blanks to complete the passage.

❶ _____________ in the past was harder for people. The way people live now has changed but some things are also similar. People in the past and now need food, ❷ _____________, and ❸ _____________.

❹ _____________ and ❺ _____________ are kinds of ❻ _____________.

At ❼ _____________ time, these crops are gathered. In the past, on ❽ _____________, people harvested crops using their hands. Now, people have machines to help them and the work has become easier. Shelter has also changed. In the past people lived in small houses. Now people also live in apartments. Our clothing has changed. Women in the past wore ❾ _____________ only. Women today wear many different kinds of colorful and interesting clothes.

09 Changes in Communication

Vocabulary

1. Fill in the blanks using the words from the box.

1.

2.

3.

4.

5.

6.

invention	tool	education	information	communication	machine

2. Choose the word that best completes the sentence.

1. __________ is how people meet new people and make new friends.

    a. Invention   b. Education   c. Machine   d. Communication

2. Nowadays people get __________ from many different newspapers, TV and the internet.

    a. education   b. information   c. machine   d. telephone

3. A car is a(n) __________ that helps people move faster.

    a. machine   b. information   c. education   d. printing press

4. The _________ of the wheel let people move fast.

   a. invention   **b.** tool   **c.** education   **d.** slate

5. At school, you learn about history, science and math. These are part of a(n) _________.

   a. telephone   **b.** invention   **c.** education   **d.** communication

6. A computer is a(n) _________ we use to work with and use the Internet.

   a. tool   **b.** slate   **c.** education   **d.** printing press

Listen & Write

ATR-SO1-W39
MP3

Listen and fill in the blanks to complete the passage.

People use ❶ _____________ to communicate. New ❷ _____________ make ❸ _____________ easier. People in the past used ❹ _____________, chalk, and ink for writing. In the present, people use computers and notebooks for writing. The telephone and ❺ _____________ are inventions that help communication. In the present, people use cellular phones to talk. The printing press is a ❻ _____________ that makes newspapers and books. In the past people got ❼ _____________ by talking to other people. Now newspapers and books are important for people to learn from. Modern communication tools such as the Internet are important to our daily life and ❽ _____________. Every day we use new inventions and important tools to help us communicate.

Vocabulary

1. **Fill in the blanks using the words from the box.**

1.

2.

3.

4.

5.

6.

| needs | wants | scarcity | money | bill | coin |

2. **Choose the word that best completes the sentence.**

1. If there is a __________ of food, people will be very hungry.

    a. penny   b. scarcity   c. coin   d. needs

2. People buy things using __________ such as paper bills and coins.

    a. money   b. wants   c. quarter   d. scarcity

3. New toys, expensive shoes and computer games are all __________.

    a. coin   b. quarter   c. money   d. wants

4. Water, food and clothes are all __________.

    a. needs   **b.** wants   **c.** penny   **d.** money

5. Some money is made of metal, these are called __________ money.

    a. scarcity   **b.** bill   **c.** coin   **d.** needs

6. We can buy more with a __________ than with a coin.

    a. bill   **b.** quarter   **c.** penny   **d.** money

Listen & Write

ATR-SO1-W40
MP3

Listen and fill in the blanks to complete the passage.

People have needs and wants. ❶ _____________ are things we must have to live. Food, shelter, and clothes are needs. ❷ _____________ are things we would like to have. Dolls and candy are wants. We use ❸ _____________ to buy what we need and want. There are different types of money. ❹ _____________ and ❺ _____________ are types of money. A bill has more value than a coin. A coin is money made of metal. There are many types of coin. A ❻ _____________ and a ❼ _____________ are two kinds of coin in America. Sometimes there is not much of something. This is called a ❽ _____________. We do not always have enough money to buy all we want. That's why we have to choose between things.

11 Goods and Services

1. Fill in the blanks using the words from the box.

1.

2.

3.

4.

5.

6.

goods	service	price	sell	buy	trade

2. Choose the word that best completes the sentence.

1. In a hospital or a post office the help you get is a __________.

   a. goods   **b.** buy   **c.** service   **d.** sell

2. You must __________ money to receive goods or services.

   a. pay   **b.** sell   **c.** grow   **d.** compare

3. Supermarkets __________ many different kinds of fruit, vegetables and snacks.

   a. pay   **b.** grow   **c.** price   **d.** sell

4. The __________ of a can of cola is usually about 1 dollar.

    a. goods   **b.** price   **c.** trade   **d.** sell

5. Before buying something you should __________ the price.

    a. buy   **b.** grow   **c.** service   **d.** compare

6. You can __________ meat at a butcher's store.

    a. buy   **b.** trade   **c.** service   **d.** pay

Listen & Write

ATR-SO1-W41
MP3

Listen and fill in the blanks to complete the passage.

People buy ❶ __________ and ❷ __________ to meet their wants and needs. Bread, apples, cars, and toys are all goods. You get services when you take a bus, go to a hairstylist, or see a doctor. People make or ❸ __________ goods and ❹ __________ them in stores. They sell services too. They sometimes come to you with their services. A mail carrier delivers your letters to you. You have to ❺ __________ money to ❻ __________ goods and services. When you do this, you should ❼ __________ the ❽ __________ and quality. You can also ❾ __________ goods or services. Children at times trade their lunch or small chores with each other.

12 Spending and Saving

1. **Fill in the blanks using the words from the box.**

1.

2.

3.

4.

5.

6.

| spend | save | cost | item | grocery | bank |

2. **Choose the word that best completes the sentence.**

1. A(n) _________ is a place where adults keep their money safe.

    a. item   **b.** bank   **c.** save   **d.** grocery

2. At the supermarket you _________ money on goods.

    a. spend   **b.** bank   **c.** cost   **d.** save

3. If you want to buy expensive goods, you must first _________ your money.

    a. bank   **b.** piggy bank   **c.** cost   **d.** save

4. Before you go shopping you should write every _________ you want
on a list.

    a. bank   **b.** spend   **c.** item   **d.** grocery

5. When you are shopping a _________ helps you remember what you
want.

    a. shopping list   **b.** save   **c.** spend   **d.** piggy bank

6. I cannot buy the doll because the _________ is too high.

    a. save   **b.** cost   **c.** bank   **d.** item

Listen & Write

ATR-SO1-W42
MP3

Listen and fill in the blanks to complete the passage.

Spending and saving money is fun to learn about. If you want to buy
food and other items, you must ❶ _____________ money. But before
you go to a ❷ _____________ store, you should make a ❸ ____________.
Write all the ❹ _____________ you need or want to buy. Then think
if you really need or want them. You should make choices about
what to buy, because you do not always have enough money. You
should choose goods after you look at their ❺ ____________. People
spend money, and people also ❻ _____________ money. Your parents
save their money in a ❼ _____________. You can save your money in a
❽ ____________. You can save money to use later.

13 Here on Earth

1. **Fill in the blanks using the words from the box.**

1.

2.

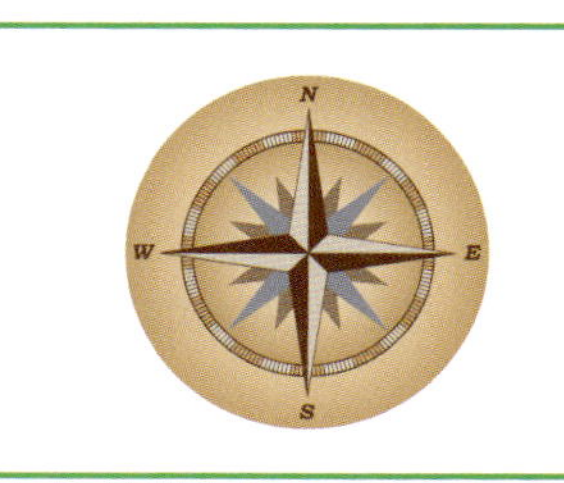

3.

4.

5.

6.

Earth	globe	land	ocean	continent	compass rose

2. **Choose the word that best completes the sentence.**

1. A __________ is a round model of our Earth.

   a. water   **b.** continent   **c.** compass rose   **d.** globe

2. The Atlantic __________ is between Europe and North America.

   a. Land   **b.** Ocean   **c.** Globe   **d.** Continent

3. Using a(n) __________, we can find north, south, east and west.

   a. compass rose   **b.** continent   **c.** air   **d.** ocean

4. Canada and the United States of America are on the North American
_________.

    a. ocean   **b.** air   **c.** water   **d.** continent

5. The _________ is home to many plants and animals.

    a. continent   **b.** earth   **c.** compass rose   **d.** rose

6. Most plants grow from the _________.

    a. compass rose   **b.** globe   **c.** land   **d.** ocean

Listen & Write

ATR-SO1-W43
MP3

Listen and fill in the blanks to complete the passage.

The planet where we live is called ❶ _____________. It is made up of
air, water, and ❷ _____________. A very large area of land is called a
❸ _____________. North America is a continent where most people
speak English. On Earth, there is more water than land. An
❹ _____________ is a large body of salt water. If the Earth is so big,
how can we find new places? A ❺ _____________, ❻ _____________,
and map are things we can use to discover places on the Earth. We
can use a globe to plan our trip. Then we should use a compass rose
and a map to find our direction. Take a look at a globe, try and plan
a trip to a fun new continent.

14 Weather and Seasons

1. Fill in the blanks using the words from the box.

1.

2.

3.

4.

5.

6.

| weather | season | spring | summer | fall | winter |

2. Choose the word that best completes the sentence.

1. In __________ the weather becomes warmer and plants become colorful.

    a. cloud   **b.** season   **c.** spring   **d.** winter

2. In __________ the weather becomes colder and animals get ready for winter.

    a. spring   **b.** temperature   **c.** summer   **d.** fall

3. The __________ in summer is very high.

    a. temperature   **b.** winter   **c.** cloud   **d.** fall

4. When the __________ is warm and sunny we can play outside.

    a. weather   **b.** spring   **c.** cloud   **d.** fall

5. Every __________ has different weather and special colors.

    a. cloud   **b.** season   **c.** spring   **d.** winter

6. In __________ snow arrives and you should dress warm.

    a. winter   **b.** cloud   **c.** summer   **d.** weather

Listen & Write

ATR-SO1-W44
MP3

Listen and fill in the blanks to complete the passage.

We have four seasons every year. Every ❶ ____________ has different ❷ ____________. The weather affects how we dress and how we live. In ❸ ____________ the ❹ ____________ is very low. The weather is cold and we need to dress warm in scarves and gloves. In ❺ ____________, the weather is warmer. Animals come out of their homes and flowers bloom. In ❻ ____________, the weather is very hot and there is a lot of daylight. In summer, there are a lot of ❼ ____________. Dark clouds mean rain. In summer, people enjoy playing outside and swimming in the ocean. In ❽ ____________, the weather is cooler and leaves fall from the trees. In fall, people and animals prepare for the cold winter.

Vocabulary

1. **Fill in the blanks using the words from the box.**

1.

2.

3.

4.

5.

6.

mountain	plain	desert	river	valley	lake

2. **Choose the word that best completes the sentence.**

1. Mount Everest is the highest _________ in the world.

   a. plain   **b.** valley   **c.** mountain   **d.** lake

2. Small rivers run from the mountain down into the _________.

   a. cloud   **b.** island   **c.** desert   **d.** valley

3. In the summer I go swimming with my friends in the _________.

   a. lake   **b.** mountain   **c.** plain   **d.** hill

4. My dad likes to go fishing in the __________.

    a. desert   **b.** plain   **c.** river   **d.** valley

5. Not many plants grow in the __________ and it does not rain often.

    a. hill   **b.** desert   **c.** lake   **d.** plain

6. Japan is a(n) __________ country in East Asia.

    a. hill   **b.** desert   **c.** island   **d.** valley

Listen & Write

ATR-SO1-W45
MP3

Listen and fill in the blanks to complete the passage.

There are many different types of land and water. A ❶ ____________ is the highest kind of land. A ❷ ____________ is also high but it is smaller than a mountain. There are low ❸ ____________ between mountains and hills. ❹ ____________ flow toward the ocean. They sometimes go through flat ❺ ____________. We can grow many kinds of food on plains whether they are high or low. We cannot grow food in a dry ❻ ____________. A ❼ ____________, another area of water, has land all around it, so it doesn't flow to the ocean like a river. An ❽ ____________ is the opposite of a lake. It is an area of land with water all around.

American Textbook Reading

Social Studies 1

WorldCom Edu www.wcbooks.co.kr